WRITING AND PRODUCING FOR TELEVISION AND FILM

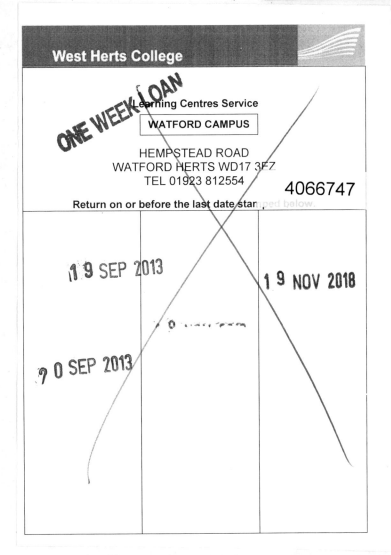
Watford Campus Library

WRITING AND PRODUCING FOR TELEVISION AND FILM

Communication for Behavior Change, Volume 2

Esta de Fossard
John Riber

Sage Publications
New Delhi ✄ Thousand Oaks ✄ London

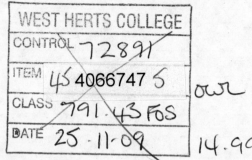
Copyright © Esta de Fossard and John Riber, 2005

First published in 2005 by

Sage Publications India Pvt Ltd
B1/I1, Mohan Cooperative Industrial Area
Mathura Road
New Delhi 110 044
www.sagepub.in

Sage Publications Inc
2455 Teller Road
Thousand Oaks, California 91320

Sage Publications Ltd
1 Oliver's Yard, 55 City Road
London EC1Y 1SP

Published by Tejeshwar Singh for Sage Publications India Pvt Ltd, phototypeset in 10.5/12.5 BruseOldStyle BT by Star Compugraphics Private Limited, Delhi and printed at Chaman Enterprises, New Delhi.

Fifth Printing 2008

Library of Congress Cataloging-in-Publication Data

De Fossard, Esta.
    Writing and producing for television and film/Esta de Fossard, John Riber.
        p. cm.—(Communication for behavior change; v. 2)
    1. Television authorship.   2. Television—Production and direction.   3. Motion picture authorship.
4. Motion pictures—Production and direction.   I. Riber, John.   II. Title.   III. Series.

PN1992.7D4   808'.066791—dc22   2005   2005023326

ISBN: 10: 0-7619-3400-6 (Pb)   10: 81-7829-551-2 (India-Pb)
            13: 978-0-7619-3400-4 (Pb)   13: 978-81-7829-551-0 (India-Pb)

Sage Production Team: Anamika Mukharji, Girish Sharma, Rajib Chatterjee, and Santosh Rawat

CONTENTS

Part 3
For the Writer

Part 4
For the Producer, Director, and Filmmaker

Part 5
For the Actors/Artists

Part 6
For the Evaluators

Part 7
For All Project Participants

PREFACE

This book is intended as a guide on the use of the visual media for Behavior Change Communication. It is not intended as a text book for those just entering the world of television or film writing and production. While there are some reminders of good writing and production techniques for many programming types, the emphasis is on what needs to be taken into account when designing, writing and producing programs that have a specific behavior change objective.

Acknowledgements

Special thanks are due to my husband, Harvey Nelson, who has contributed most of the photographs for the book, and whose constant interest in my work, readiness to travel with me to all corners of the globe, and willingness to answer my endless questions inspire me to keep going.

I would also like to thank the many friends (writers, producers, actors, program managers) I have made around the world whose interest in Entertainment–Education and eagerness to learn about it and put it into practice has motivated me to put ideas into printed words.

Finally, I must thank my wonderful editor at Sage Publications—Anamika Mukharji—whose dedication, hard work, and delightful sense of humor have made working with her a delight.

Thank you all.

Esta de Fossard

I would like to thank my wife Louise who gives me far too much credit for what we have together achieved.

Thanks to my mentor, the late Dr Andreas Fugelsang, whose work continues to inspire me to pursue the challenges of learning from those I am supposed to be teaching.

I also thank three institutions: Media For Development Trust, Zimbabwe; Media For Development International, USA; and Worldview International Foundation, Bangladesh that created the possibility for me to do what I need to do.

John Riber

PART 1

Entertainment–Education

1

USING TELEVISION AND FILM FOR SOCIAL DEVELOPMENT
The Entertainment–Education Format

Photograph by John Riber

The visual medium has tremendous mass appeal and can attract large audiences.

POPULARITY OF THE VISUAL MEDIA

In the modern world, the visual media (film and television) are universally popular and are becoming increasingly available in developing countries. People everywhere love to go to a movie or to watch a TV show. It seems valid, therefore, to consider employing these media as part of a Behavior Change Communication project to encourage positive social change in individuals and societies.

There is no denying the popularity of television. In remote rural areas of developing countries where individual television ownership is virtually unknown, television programs can still be seen through the medium of the video van. Many development projects make use of video-vans on a regular basis, and the video showings always attract a great deal of interest. The presentation of well-made social development programs through video vans or through television can be a very powerful motivator of behavior change. Even in places where both film and television are part of everyday life, there is a continuing attraction to the visual media that cannot and should not be denied. Indeed, as Miguel Sabido says, "television has become the big moral guide in today's world" (Sabido 1999).* While words alone (radio, print, oral storytelling) can be compelling because of their appeal to the imagination, it remains true that in many cases "a picture is worth a thousand words." Television and film can present visual role models who spark in viewers the will to emulate desired behavior change. The visual media can **demonstrate** to the chosen audience exactly how to undertake activities that can improve their lives and the visual media can **show** an audience, in inspiring pictures, how their lives can be bettered as a result of making changes.

---

*Miguel Sabido. 1999. "Social Uses of Commercial Soap Operas", *Journal of Development Communication*, Vol. 10.

For example, a film that carries a message on the advantages of proper nutrition for children can show, graphically and dramatically, a comparison between the appearance, health and demeanor of children who are properly fed and those who are not. The prospect of the same positive health and appearance being possible in their own children can be a powerful motivator in encouraging audience members to change behavior.

THE ENTERTAINMENT–EDUCATION FORMAT

There are many ways of using visual media to bring important knowledge to audiences. Jingles, spots, and advertisements are commonly used to remind viewers of such things as the immunization days or the importance of Vitamin A. Documentaries can present audiences with impressive facts such as how new farming methods can increase their crop production.

Perhaps the most powerful use of television or film for motivating social development is the Entertainment–Education format. "Entertainment–Education is the process of purposively designing and implementing a media message both to entertain and educate, in order to increase audience members' knowledge about an educational issue, create favorable attitudes, and change overt behavior" (Singhal and Rogers 1999).[*] In other words, the Entertainment–Education format combines an engaging form of entertainment with a relevant educational message. Entertainment appeals to the **emotions** of the audience. Once the audience is engrossed in the entertainment, the relevant educational message can be blended in gradually, naturally, and subtly. The educational message appeals to the **mind** and the **logic** of the audience. The Entertainment–Education format, therefore, employs a combination of emotional appeal and relevant knowledge to demonstrate and communicate the benefits that can result from a change in personal behavior and social norms.

> Entertainment = Emotional appeal
> Education = Relevant knowledge

At the same time, it must be remembered that the Entertainment–Education format is not a guarantee of behavior change and there are those who are likely to oppose its use. The most common criticisms of the format are:

---

[*]Arvind Singhal and Everett M. Rogers. 1999. *Entertainment–Education: A Communication Strategy for Social Change*. London: Lawrence Erlbaum Associates.

- It is expensive when film or TV is the medium being used. The creation of a film or TV drama serial does cost money, and there are those who will argue that the money could be better spent on cheaper methods of knowledge dissemination, such as print or face-to-face discussion.
- Many of the most common behavior change topics are considered inappropriate or too sensitive to show on public airwaves. Such topics as safe childbirth, HIV and AIDS prevention, Adolescent Reproductive Health, etc., do require fairly direct discussion of personal matters and some cultures are not comfortable with such topics being shown on television or even in cinemas.
- There are critics who are concerned that writers, directors and others might enter into the Entertainment–Education field for the wrong reasons: to draw attention and fame towards themselves.

All those involved in an Entertainment–Education project should be aware of the possible weaknesses of the format and be prepared to offset these weaknesses whenever necessary. The likely criticisms should be kept in mind when planning an Entertainment–Education project. Response to these particular criticisms might suggest:

- While the creation of visual media is expensive, it can be re-used in many ways. Well-made dramas can be re-broadcast or re-shown many times using video vans in remote areas of the country.
- Careful message creation can avoid the problem of offending the media outlets. Including media policy makers in the message design is an essential first step in ensuring that programs will be approved and shown. Careful writing is another important aspect in overcoming this criticism. By their presence at the Design Workshop (see Chapter 3), writers can learn from the policy makers just what can be said and shown. They can learn from audience members and content specialists how to provide essential information in a non-offensive manner.
- Commitment to the goals of the Entertainment–Education project is a prerequisite for all those involved in it. This is particularly true of those involved in the creative aspect of the project. They should understand from the outset that the project is not about making them famous, but about improving the lives of ordinary people.
- A further important consideration is that the Entertainment–Education medium (be it film, television, community theater) should never be a stand-alone product. There should always be other interventions to support and replicate the messages it delivers. The main asset of Entertainment–Education is that it reaches out primarily to people's emotions and thus engages their attention to learn more about the recommended behavior change.

DRAMA

There are several ways in which the Entertainment–Education format can be used; perhaps the most popular of these is drama. All the world loves a good story. A drama is a story that is acted out in front of the audience by a number of actors (either on a stage or on a screen), rather than being told to them by one narrator or storyteller.

The Advantages of Drama

- Drama can be entertaining; that is, it can attract and hold the attention of an audience.
- It can provide the audience with vicarious emotional experiences, allowing them to feel and express emotions that they might otherwise have to repress in real life.
  For example, they can express open anger at a political "character" in a drama in a way that would be impossible, or even dangerous, in real life.
- The characters of a drama can act as role models and demonstrate the benefits of the proposed behavior change in a natural way.
- Audiences can see people like themselves and with lives like their own learning about, considering, accepting and even advocating social change, thereby providing a powerful call to action.
- Visual drama can reach audiences who are illiterate or semi-literate.

Types of Drama

Drama usually occurs in one of three forms: the stand-alone drama; the drama series; the drama serial.

The Stand-alone Drama

This is complete in one showing. Like the average movie, the stand-alone drama is typically 60–90 minutes long and contains one major plot.

The Drama Series

This is a collection of short dramas (typically each drama in the series is 20 or 30 minutes long) broadcast on a weekly basis. The same main characters appear in each program of the series, but they are engaged in a separate and complete plot (story) every week. The drama series can be compared to a regular newspaper comic strip: the same characters appear every week, but they are involved in a different activity each time they appear. (The Design Document sample that is given in Appendix B was created for a drama series.)

The Drama Serial

This is an ongoing story divided into episodes (much like the chapters of a novel) that are shown on air regularly: day by day or week by week for a period of six months, a year or even more. At the end of each episode the story is left incomplete, closing on a question or a note of suspense so that viewers are encouraged to watch the following episode to find out what will happen next. Typically the Entertainment–Education drama is shown at the rate of one episode per week for 6–12 months. In some cases the drama is extended and becomes a part of regular entertainment for viewers. The famous, award-winning South African series *Soul City* has been on the air since 1994 with a once-a-week TV serial. In the last few years the social change efforts of this series have been enhanced by a radio drama that is aired every day, and the addition of a children's television and radio series, *Soul Buddyz*.*

Any of these drama formats—the stand-alone drama, the drama series or the drama serial—can be comic, tragic, mysterious, adventurous or can combine two or more of these emotions. The serial drama, which usually contains three or more separate plots, can represent a number of emotions so that it can be, for example, tragic in one plot, amusing in another (which might also contain a love story) and frightening in yet a third plot. Similarly these separate plots can be designed to appeal to different audiences (adolescents, rural workers, city dwellers) but subtly blended in a way that gives the message universal relevance.

Drama is, therefore, a powerful medium through which to demonstrate positive social change to an audience and to encourage audience members to improve their lives by making this change themselves. It must be understood, however, that behavior change drama (or Entertainment–Education drama) is different in a number of ways from drama designed purely for entertainment. The major difference is the natural and subtle integration of the accurate educational message into the entertaining story, and in order for this to be successful, there must be careful planning from the outset of the project.

---

*The Soul City Institute for Health and Development, led by its founder, Garth Japhet, is a non-governmental organization based in Johannesburg, South Africa. Known generally as Soul City, the institute was established in 1992 to employ mass media—especially Entertainment–Education dramas—for health improvement and social development. Details of the program types and the remarkable success of Soul City can be found on *www.soulcity.org*.

STARTING UP THE SOCIAL DEVELOPMENT PROJECT

Steps in the Entertainment–Education Project Development

Film or television drama (or other types of programming) for a social development project can be initiated in one of two ways: by the Behavior Change Communication (BCC) project management or by the independent video or filmmaker. In either case, the film or television project is developed through a series of steps that are demonstrated by the 10 carriages of the A train (see Figure 1.1): Audience; Analysis; Access; Articulation; Artistry; Auxiliaries; Advocacy; Advertising; Assessment; Adjustment.

Each of the carriages represents an essential element of project development and all elements (carriages) must be linked securely and smoothly. The train runs on the wheels of competent Administration, led by the program manager or executive producer. The 10 main steps in an Entertainment–Education project development are as follows:

1. Audience

Any project that aims to change social norms relies on, and is led throughout its development by a thorough, precise and empathetic understanding of the audience(s) for which it is intended. A detailed analysis of the geographic, demographic, economic, cultural and social factors that shape audience behavior is necessary. These factors can include current knowledge, attitudes, practices, and methods of advocacy related to the desired change. Other important factors include age, sex, literacy, income, personality, lifestyle, cultural and social values, individual and community variables and media exposure, etc. Only a very close understanding of the audience(s) whose lives can be improved by behavior change can help to determine the behavior change theories, specific motivators and role models that can be used to encourage change.

2. Analysis

Changing health behavior or other types of knowledge, attitudes, and practice through a communication strategy requires accurate information and in-depth analysis of several important factors:

The problem
There must be a clear and carefully researched analysis of what the project directors see as the problem to be addressed. This analysis can be started by a review of existing health and demographic data, survey results, study findings, etc. It should be enhanced by specific base-line research of the problem, to help determine the causes and the real possibility of bringing about change. If, for example, resources such as health clinics are

Figure 1.1

The "A Train" Pattern for Social Development Drama

required for the change, and they are not available to the audience, then no amount of behavior change communication will be effective. Similarly, effecting change can be extremely challenging if the current behavior is based on long-held cultural or religious beliefs.

Existing programs, policies, and resources

A review of existing relevant social change policies is necessary to learn what is legal and acceptable to the current government. Equally important is determining what other programs already exist, whether run by the government or Non-Government Organizations (NGOs), so that duplication can be avoided and partnerships can be established. It is vital to understand where and what supplies are available, what services and resources are on hand and what is still needed.

3. Access

Once it is determined that the problem can and should be addressed through behavior change communication, it is important to establish that there is ready access to all the facilities and people needed to help ensure project success.

- **Communication capacity:** It is necessary to examine local communication capacity—accessibility of suitable production houses, artists, shooting locations, broadcast stations, broadcast times, etc.
- **Audience capacity:** Similarly, it is necessary to ensure that the proposed audiences have access to the communication outlet (e.g., television) or cinema that will be used.
- **Training needs:** The writing, production and presentation of Entertainment–Education programming are very different from typical entertainment work. Where this type of production has not been done previously, it might be necessary to provide training in design, writing and production of the drama. It is necessary to ensure that the project has access to and the budget to pay for training as needed.

4. Articulation

Entertainment–Education programs designed for social development require that the messages to be shared with the audience are very carefully articulated (or worded) and presented so that they are both understandable and relevant to the chosen audience(s). When creating a stand-alone film or television drama that has one main message, the job of articulating the message and how it will be included in the drama might be left to the writer. In drama serials, where there might be more than one topic, or where the scope and sequence of the message(s) must be specifically determined, it is more relevant and successful to have the message articulated carefully and precisely by a specially selected

Message Design Team. The members of this Design Team can work together during a Design Workshop to determine and record the agreed-upon message details in a Design Document which then becomes the reliable reference for all those working on the project. Chapter 3 provides details of the design team, workshop and document.

5. Artistry

The knowledge contained in the behavior change messages is of obvious importance in bringing about social change, but knowledge alone is usually not enough to motivate permanent change. Entertainment in one of many forms, including drama, can provide emotional stimulus, role modeling, and thought-provoking demonstration to evoke the motivation that knowledge alone may not be able to inspire.

In film and television, the **artistry** of the writer, the director, the actors (artists), the musicians and the film crew among others, is just as important as message articulation. The success of every Entertainment–Education project relies on harmonious blending of artistry and articulation. For this reason, it might be necessary to organize a workshop for writers, providing them with guidance on how to blend educational messages naturally and subtly into a powerfully entertaining drama. This workshop should be conducted by someone experienced in the area of Entertainment–Education writing and production. The director and actors may also need guidance on character interpretation and message delivery in order to effectively convey the message to the audience.

6. Auxiliaries

There is general agreement in the world of social development that one medium alone is usually not enough to maintain behavior change. It is always advisable to have auxiliary or support materials that will enhance the messages delivered through the primary medium. The question of what type of support materials would be most appropriate and attractive to the audiences is one that should be kept in mind from the outset of the project. When film or TV drama has been selected as the main medium, there should be careful consideration as to what other approaches might be used to encourage audience members to watch and to act on what they see. Auxiliary products might be posters, brochures, or print and audio materials making use of characters/events from the film to reassert the message. Alternatively, activities such as competitions, road shows, school visits, musical presentations, etc., might be seen as appropriate ways of encouraging viewers to recall, consider and act upon what they have seen in the TV drama serials.

7. Advocacy

The ultimate aim of social change projects is to establish new and permanent social norms, rather than just occasional individual behavior change. For this reason, the encouragement of **advocacy** is important; that is, encouraging those who view, understand, and are motivated by what they learn from the drama to share their ideas with others and encourage others to accept the changes as well. Advocacy of this nature can be demonstrated within the drama, but it can be encouraged in other ways as well. Listener groups can be established that invite people to get together to listen to the drama and discuss it after the broadcast. If funding permits, leaders from listener groups can be trained to encourage discussion and motivate group members to bring other family members and friends into the group to listen and learn with them.

Advocacy is also important in motivating community leaders and others in positions of power to believe in and encourage the desired behavior change. In some projects—such as those related to adolescent knowledge of life skills and appropriate sexual behavior—special materials (pamphlets, booklets) can be prepared to share with community and religious leaders in order to help them to understand the need for behavior change and to motivate them to support the aims of the project.

8. Advertising and Promotion

Advertising and promoting the drama are essential activities, which are usually best handled by an experienced advertising agency. Agency representatives should be present at the design workshop (see Chapter 3) and have a clear understanding of the kind of social development the project is promoting. They should also be well acquainted with the drama and its characters, in case the characters can be used in the promotional and advertising campaigns.

9. Assessment

Ongoing assessment or monitoring is always necessary, and very possible, with a drama serial. Pilot testing of the storylines and the characters should be done with two or three of the early episodes before the serial goes on the air, and appropriate changes made if necessary. In order to save money, the pilot testing can be done with audio versions of the video scripts (see sample in Chapter 12). While audio scripts do not give the full picture of what the film or TV will present, they can help determine if the audience accepts and believes in the characters, and is aware of and has interest in the important behavior changes being recommended.

Once the drama serial is on the air, regular monitoring can be carried out through Listener Groups, focus group discussions, or requests for feedback from viewers. Even if several episodes have been completed (recorded and edited) in advance of going on the air, it is always possible to make small changes if the ongoing assessment shows this to be necessary. However, if the whole project has been carefully planned, and if there have been adequate pilot tests, it is usually not necessary to make any drastic changes as the drama moves forward.

10. Adjustment

Successful films and TV serial dramas often suggest, or even demand, a follow-on series. If this is possible, then one must ensure careful re-assessment of all aspects of the project so that adjustment(s) can be made, as necessary, either to the messages or the drama presentation, or to other aspects of the project. Appropriate and timely adjustment can help to maintain the success of the first presentation, or to improve upon it.

There are many people involved in the creation of a successful Entertainment–Education TV or film production. Leading the project will be the program manager or executive producer. This person can be seen, perhaps, as the chief engineer who ensures that the train is well-fueled and running smoothly and that all carriages are firmly connected.

PART 2

For the Program Manager

2

THE ROLE OF THE
PROGRAM MANAGER

Photograph by Harvey Nelson

The program manager guides the program from the outset.

The creation of successful social development films and videos requires the closest possible collaboration between the program manager and the filmmaker (or director) to ensure that accurate and appropriate messages are delivered in the most engaging manner to the selected audience(s).

The program manager (or executive producer) is the overall leader of the social change project. The program manager should be a person with previous managerial experience and a deep commitment to the goals of the Entertainment–Education project. The film or TV director should be a person with considerable experience in direction and a willingness to adapt to the needs of Entertainment–Education programming.

THE PROGRAM MANAGER'S ROLE

The overall responsibility of the program manager, who is also the executive producer, is to ensure that:

- all logistical and financial matters related to the entire process of film production are properly managed.
- the proposed film or TV drama matches the project's overall behavior change objectives.
- nothing is compromised in clearly interpreting these objectives and translating them into a filmed drama.

THE DIRECTOR'S ROLE

The **director** is the filmmaker who has overall responsibility for

- the artistic realization of the drama.
- the technical processes involved in putting the script (the story and its messages) into the film or TV format.
- ensuring that the filmed version of the story and the messages (*a*) suits the entertainment preferences of the chosen audience and (*b*) adheres meticulously to the message content and sequence as approved by the design team.

It is vital that the program manager and director understand their individual roles and responsibilities and work together cooperatively. The program manager—representing the institution creating and paying for the project—is the ultimate authority. The director—and everyone working with the director—must understand and accept this.

STARTING UP THE A TRAIN

Administration

The program manager heads the administration team and is responsible for ensuring that all necessary tasks are allocated and completed on time. Poor administration inevitably results in a weak or failed project. The program manager, therefore, should have a clear understanding of the steps to be followed in creating a successful Entertainment–Education drama. The task is challenging, but can and should be very rewarding.

The Program Manager and the A Train

The program manager's tasks in the various "carriages" of the A Train are as follows:

Audience

The program manager must know and understand the intended audience of the project, and must encourage all others working on the project to become familiar with the audience as well. Preferably, the program manager will be someone who is already familiar with the culture and lifestyle of the intended audience. Frequently, however, the person in a managerial position has a well-educated urban upbringing and might not be as familiar as necessary with the everyday realities of the lives of an intended rural audience. This can be compensated by making regular visits to areas where the audience lives and by learning to appreciate their lifestyle and their needs.

The program manager should also ensure that all others working on the project—including writers, director, and artists—are similarly encouraged to truly understand the cultural and religious background, lifestyles, needs, and concerns of members of the intended audience.

Analysis

The program manager is responsible for ensuring that the social change project is equipped at the outset with a complete analysis of the current knowledge, behavior, and needs of the chosen audience, especially with regard to the behavior to be changed. Alternatively, if such information is not already available, the program manager must contract with a research agency to conduct a baseline survey which can be used to determine existing audience knowledge and behavior.

The baseline research can also guide the Design Team in deciding which behavior change theory will make the most effective basis for the project. (See the information provided on behavior change theories on pages 57–59.)

Access

Once television or film has been determined as the major message-delivery medium, the program manager has the responsibility of exploring the local capacity for undertaking such work. Some projects require that competitive proposals be submitted by various film and television production houses. In such cases, the program manager is responsible for placing advertisements for proposals, receiving the proposals and putting together a small team to determine which of the proposals is best suited to the needs and financial capabilities of the project. In examining the proposals, the team—led by the program manager—should take into consideration:

- previous experience
- equipment availability (either the company will already possess the equipment or they should provide specific details of where and how they will acquire the equipment)
- availability of all necessary equipment at the time required by the project
- CVs of chief personnel who will be involved in the project
- samples of previous work

- access to appropriate artists (actors), musicians, etc.
- recommendations from previous clients

It will be the program manager's task to finalize contracts with the production company, artists, etc.

Some further guidelines on assessing production capacity can be found at the end of this chapter.

Articulation

The determination and articulation of the messages to be included in the Entertainment–Education drama is organized in one of two ways:

1. If the production is to be stand-alone film or a short television series concentrating on one topic, the program manager will hold a meeting (in effect a short design workshop) with the writer(s) and director and provide them with full and accurate details of the message information to be included.
2. If the project is to make use of a drama serial that will continue for many months and will cover several topics, or a range of sub-topics, the determination of message scope and sequence is usually undertaken during a week-long design workshop. It is the program manager's job to:

- set dates and location for the design workshop.
- invite participants (sample invitation letters are included in Appendix A).
- determine the agenda.
- ensure that all necessary equipment and materials are on hand.
- collect all necessary reference materials and make copies available at the workshop.
- arrange all details concerning such things as venue, accommodation, meals, etc.
- ensure that the workshop runs smoothly and that the first draft of the design document is completed.
- ensure that other important tasks (such as the appointment of the script review team and the script support team) are completed.
- arrange a follow-up writers' workshop where necessary.
- arrange and conduct a design document review meeting.
- arrange ongoing review of message content of scripts.
- arrange pilot testing of scripts to ensure acceptance of the message and suitability of story.

Full details of the design process will be found in Chapter 3.

Artistry: Writers

The program manager is responsible for deciding how the writer(s) will be selected and whether or not they will require training in Entertainment–Education methodology. If training is required, it is usually best to have it conducted right after the design workshop so that the prospective writer(s) will have knowledge of the messages to be included while preparing a story outline and character profiles.

How many writers are needed?
The question often arises as to how many writers are needed to create a TV serial drama. There is no definitive answer to this question. Some writers choose to work alone; others prefer to work as a team. Writers are selected based on their previous experience in writing for the visual media and their willingness and ability to adapt to the new format if they have no previous experience writing Entertainment–Education programs. During their interview for possible involvement in the behavior change project, they can be asked if they prefer to work alone or with a team. The determination of whether to employ one script writer or a team can also be influenced by the budget.

Team writing
If a team is employed, it is important to know how its members work together. There should be a team leader, and the team should have a precise method for splitting up the work. Either they will all work on all episodes together; or each writer will work on one plot only; or each writer will work on a group of consecutive episodes. No matter which method they choose, they must have a clearly delineated synopsis, workplan, and timeline, which should meet with the program manager's approval.

One writer
If only one writer will be employed for the scripting, it is often advisable, nevertheless, to invite more than one to the design workshop so that the final selection can be made based on their interest in and responses to the requirements of the project. Each writer can be invited to prepare an audition script at the end of the design workshop. The audition script will be a brief synopsis or treatment of the whole drama story together with one complete script. (See Chapter 4.)

Following the selection of the writer(s), the program manager should complete the writing contract, ensuring that the writer(s) will agree with the established timeline and required standard of work.

Actors
As well as selecting and contracting for script writing, the program manager should ensure that the chosen production house engages appropriate artists (actors) for the drama. Usually, the artists are put under contract to the production house, but some

funding bodies prefer that the artists are contracted directly by the management of the behavior change project. It is often a good idea for the program manager to ask the production company to provide an audition tape that demonstrates the talent of the artists as well as their suitability for roles in the drama and their appropriateness for the chosen audience.

For example, it can be a mistake to cast a young, extremely beautiful, and famous actress in the role of a rural health volunteer. The audience will find it hard to believe in this character if she looks very different from the health workers to whom they are accustomed.

Auxiliaries

Other forms of artistry include art work for brochures and other print materials. The program manager is also in charge of the development of these materials, whether this is done by people on the project staff, or through a contract with an outside agency. It is helpful to determine early in the project if there are existing materials that could be used (without alteration) to support the television or film. It is not uncommon for other non-government organizations (NGOs) to have, for example, print materials (such as brochures) that can be used or adapted inexpensively for the current project.

Where previously prepared materials are available, these should be brought to the design workshop so that the program messages, if appropriate, can be tailored to match them.

If new materials are to be designed to accompany the television programs, the nature of these should be considered throughout the workshop so that references to them can be made as necessary throughout the programs.

Great care should be taken to determine whether support materials are necessary, and if they are, to ensure that what is created is appropriate for and easily obtained and used by the audience.

Advocacy

The importance of advocacy in behavior change cannot be overstressed. The drama itself should encourage viewers to talk about the story and its messages with others. This is achieved most easily if the story is so engaging that viewers want to talk about it. Encouraging advocacy among viewers is the task of the creative writers. Encouraging advocacy among community leaders and others is the work of the project team, under the leadership of the program manager.

During the analysis phase of the project, determinations should be made about who the important stakeholders are, and which community leaders should be encouraged to support and spread the word about the messages being disseminated. Sometimes the most important advocates are government policymakers, sometimes local community leaders, sometimes religious leaders, sometimes educators, and sometimes several or all of these.

It might be necessary in some cases to hold explanatory meetings or create special print materials to assist leaders to understand the message and its importance. For example, in some countries public discussion of any sex-related subject is strictly taboo. The HIV and AIDS pandemic, however, virtually demands that references be made to sexual behavior when encouraging protection from the disease. It can be beneficial to share intended materials with political, community, and religious leaders in advance, and provide them with clear explanations of why certain approaches to the subject must be used. Getting their support to advocate the changes being recommended in the drama can have a major and positive effect on the success of the programs. The program manager will have the task of helping to determine what advocacy actions and materials are needed and of ensuring that these are created and delivered on time and to the right people.

Advertising and Promotion

Usually the most successful way of attracting audience attention to the programs and to their messages is through commercials created by a professional advertising agency. It is necessary, however, that the agency has a full and clear understanding of the purpose and intention of the project as a humanitarian and not a commercial enterprise. The program manager must ensure that all advertising and promotion materials are in line with the fundamental objectives of the project, and that they do not misrepresent the project or the audience in any way.

The timing of advertising and promotion ahead of broadcast dates, and how often and when they should continue during the on-air period must be given careful consideration. Initial discussion of these matters can be held during the design workshop. It is always advantageous to have representatives of the selected advertising agency present during at least part of the design workshop so that they can obtain a clear and accurate picture of the project intentions.

Assessment

The researcher (or research team) will be responsible for monitoring and evaluating the effect of the programs on the intended audience. The program manager should ensure that the researchers allow for ongoing assessment while the programs are on air, and for summative evaluation when all programs have been broadcast. Research, monitoring and evaluation can be time-consuming and expensive, but these are essential parts of any behavior change project and the program manager should ensure that research work is done effectively and on time. A full report on all aspects of research, monitoring, and evaluation should be prepared at the end of the project to (*a*) provide justification for the project and (*b*) provide guidelines for future projects of the same nature. It is the program manager's job to ensure, not only that all research and evaluation work is being done at the right time, but also that full and accurate reporting of the findings is presented when the project is complete.

Adjustment

The biggest contribution the program manager can make to the development of future projects is the maintenance of full and complete reports of project activities, together with "lessons learned" and "recommendations for future projects." Accurate reporting, therefore, is a major part of the program manager's job. Together with evaluation results, these reports can go a long way in determining what adjustments should be made if the project is to be continued, or if it is to develop into something new or different.

ANALYZING COMMUNICATION CAPACITY

Important Questions

Before deciding to work on a TV or film project for social development, it is important for the program manager to assess the local availability, reach, and costs of the chosen medium, and to identify audience viewing habits and media access. Important questions to be considered address matters such as

Cost
The cost of creating, producing, distributing and airing visual media is much higher than either audio or print.

Question
Is there a budget large enough to allow for film or television production?
The program manager should obtain reliable quotes from various companies before a final decision is made regarding the use of visual media.

Pictorial needs
Unlike radio programs and books that leave visual imagery to the imagination of the audience, television and film leave no doubt in the minds of the viewers about such matters as:

- physical appearance of the characters.
- quality and characteristics of buildings (homes, etc.) where the action is occurring.

- cultural bias (very often revealed by such elements as clothes, food, and living environment). Where radio or print allow the audience to imagine faces and surroundings to be much like their own, visual media present viewers with a fixed, definite image.

Question
Is the specific audience chosen sufficiently large and autonomous to justify the making of a film or video, or are there too many diverse ethnic groups to be reached through a video drama or film?
(This question is particularly important in countries where there is a wide diversity of ethnic groups and religions.)

Casting
Make-up can help a young person look old, but it is virtually impossible to cast an adult in the role of a child, or a plump elderly man as a twenty-year old athlete.

Questions
Is there a ready pool of experienced actors who can be called upon to create a quality drama?
If actors are available, but they have no previous television or film experience, is it possible within the timeframe and the budget constraints to provide appropriate training, keeping in mind that acting for film or television is very different from stage or radio acting?

International standards
Almost every country in the world has access to internationally made films and television programs. Even if the storylines of these films are not very good, the quality of cinematography, editing, casting and special effects is generally at least professional, if not outstanding. Audiences everywhere are accustomed to certain standards in both film and television. While local productions most certainly hold considerable appeal for local audiences, these international standards put a burden on local writers, producers and directors to create programs that at least *look* as good as commonly seen international programs.

Questions
Is there a local production company that has previous experience with filming drama? Or is there a local director who has this experience and who could work with a local film company to create a product that will attract a local audience even if international films are available at the same time?

Director's role
Historically, the film director has always been the person who makes the creative and final decisions about how the various scenes in the film will be interpreted and acted

and where they will be set. Directors are accustomed to having the liberty to adjust the story to suit their interpretation of it and their personal artistic inclinations. With an Entertainment–Education drama, however, such freedom can be disastrous if it allows the director to alter or destroy the intended message or the focus of the drama. The director, therefore, must believe in the importance of the intended behavior change and the value of the TV or film project in helping to achieve this change. Moreover, the director must be willing to work in the closest possible cooperation with the program manager.

Questions

Is there an experienced, competent director who is willing to adapt to the Entertainment–Education style of direction and willing to allow the program manager to have the last word?

Will it be necessary to establish a contract that spells out the need for the director to follow the requirements of the design document and to accept the program director's word as final?

Writer's role

It can be equally difficult to find writers who have had any previous experience at writing Entertainment–Education drama. Well-known and successful writers of dramas designed solely for entertainment are often unwilling or unable to change their style to suit the needs of Entertainment–Education writing. This change in style requires, first, a total commitment to the importance of the messages in the drama, and second, a willingness to adhere to the message scope and sequence of the design document.

Question

Is it possible to locate a writer or writers willing to learn the Entertainment–Education format and writing style? They can do this either by studying a book on Entertainment–Education script writing (such as this one) or by attending a workshop arranged by the project and conducted by an expert in Entertainment–Education writing.

Entertainment perspective

Most people are accustomed to using film and television as a means of escape from their everyday lives. They expect to be entertained by what they are watching, and are quite likely to switch to another channel or turn off the set if they are faced with what seems like a lecture or a classroom.

Questions

What is the current experience of the chosen audience with regard to film and television? Will they expect entertainment to predominate in their programming? If so, the project must be especially particular about answering the question: is it possible to find all the necessary top quality people for every phase of the film development?

None of these challenges are insurmountable, but all must be carefully examined during the analysis phase of the communication project. When these questions and all other questions pertaining to assessment have been satisfactorily answered, it is possible to move to the next stage: message articulation.

3

ARTICULATION

Designing Message Content for Entertainment–Education Programs

Successful message delivery requires close cooperation of all members of the Design Team, including the director and the program manager.

SPECIFIC MESSAGE DESIGN

Creating films or TV dramas for social change purposes involves two levels of design: overall project design and specific message design or **articulation**. Once all aspects of basic project design have been satisfactorily accomplished, the business of specific message design can commence.

The close cooperation between the program manager and the director really begins with their contribution to the articulation stage. While the program manager brings a special understanding of what needs to be communicated to which audience and why, the director brings a special understanding of how the message can be best communicated to the chosen audience using a visual medium. Both the program manager and the director are essential members of the design team and they can demonstrate their cooperative approach to the project during the design workshop.

THE DESIGN PROCESS

As already noted, Entertainment–Education drama is a blend of two equally important components: the drama and the message. The drama story (the plot and the characters) provides the entertainment and the message provides the education. The creation and presentation of the drama's entertaining story is in the hands of the writer, the actors and director; the compilation of the educational message is the work of the design team.

Drama = Entertainment	Message = Education
Drama = Writer	Message = Design Team

An Entertainment–Education drama that hopes to motivate positive social change must be meticulously designed with regard to the message(s) it will convey. Leaving the writer(s) to determine how the message(s) is to be integrated can work if the drama concentrates on one topic only. Similarly, this approach can be effective if the aim of the drama is primarily to encourage interest in the recommended change, and where there will be no follow-up measurement to determine if actual, precise behavior change has occurred in the viewing population.

However, some projects are designed to effect behavior change in a number of areas, such as all areas of basic family health, or all areas of adolescent life skills, and to scientifically measure the change in knowledge and behavior that results from the drama. In such cases, it is unfair and unwise to leave message specification to the writer(s) alone. Under these circumstances, it is best to adopt a careful design process made up of three main elements:

- the design team
- the design workshop
- the design document

THE DESIGN TEAM

It is the program manager's responsibility to organize each step in the specific message design, beginning with the selection of members of the **design team**. For a social development film or television project, the team should include the following people:

Essential Design Team Members

- the program manager
- content specialists: those knowledgeable about the technical or educational information to be disseminated to the chosen audience
- audience representatives: actual members of the selected audience(s) or those closely associated with the chosen audience and knowledgeable about their current practices and attitudes in relation to the desired behavior change
- ministry representatives where necessary: those who can speak for relevant government policies, such as the Ministry of Health and the Ministry of Information
- the film or television director
- media outlet representative: someone who can ensure that messages are designed in such a way that the drama will not be pulled off the air for being offensive
- the writer or writers
- research representative: someone who was involved in the base line research that will provide the foundation for all decisions involving the objectives of the project

In particular cases there might be others who should be involved in the team as well, such as

- representatives of NGOs involved in similar activities or able to assist in the support and dissemination of the project
- a resource representative who can ensure that resources (such as clinics, trained birth attendants or even vitamin pills) needed by the audience are available
- a language specialist who can assist with translating technical terminology into dialect easily understood by the chosen audience
- a promotion manager or representative of the organization that has been hired to prepare and develop a full promotional plan to support the messages of the video component (A separate promotion manager is not essential and is usually used only with a project that is undertaking a major campaign of which the video project is one small component.)
- Support materials creator(s): if it is proposed that specific support materials will be made and used with the drama, the person(s) appointed to prepare these materials should also attend the design workshop

Inviting Design Team Members

Dates for the design workshop should be determined well in advance to increase the chances of having all necessary team members present. Invitations to the design workshop should be sent in good time and should be accompanied by a brief but clear explanation of the objectives and importance of the workshop. (See Sample Letters in Appendix A: Preparing for the Design Workshop.)

THE DESIGN WORKSHOP

The design workshop is the meeting at which the members of the design team make all necessary determinations about the messages to be presented in the drama. The design meeting for a stand-alone film might require just a couple of days' work. The design workshop for a television serial of 13–26 episodes typically lasts from several days to a full week (or more) depending on the nature of the project being designed.

It can be advantageous to hold the Design Workshop at an out-of-town location where all team members will "live in" for the duration of the workshop. This arrangement avoids the problem of team members missing part of the workshop in order to go their offices or attend other business. The satisfactory completion of the design document depends on all team members being present throughout the workshop.

It is also a good idea very often to invite participants to a first-night meeting and dinner, the day before the actual workshop is to begin. This helps to ensure that all participants will be present when the real work of program design begins the following morning.

Design Workshop Needs

The number of people attending the workshop varies from 15 to 30, so for plenary sessions it is necessary to have a good-sized meeting room. There should also be room for small groups to sit and work together, either in the plenary room or in smaller adjacent rooms. Suggested facilities and equipment required for the workshop can be found in Appendix A.

While all facilitators will have their own methods of running the design workshop, the agenda that follows can be considered by those who are preparing for a drama serial of 26 episodes or more.

Design Workshop Agenda

Opening night
Participants arrive
Introductory welcome and presentation

Introduction of facilitators
Introduction of participants
Dinner
Getting to know each other time

Day 1

8:00 AM   PLENARY
             Program Manager:
             Introduction and overview of Workshop Objectives;
             Select reporters for following morning
             Workshop Facilitator:
             Overview of goals of Behavior Change Communication
             Introduction of Entertainment–Education format
             Introduction to Design Process:

             Design Team
             Design Workshop
             Design Document

10:30 AM   TEA BREAK

11:00 AM   *Workshop Facilitator:*
             Overview of components of the Design Document
             Research Group:
             Point 1 of Design Document Justification (research findings):
             Discussion and questions from participants

1:00 PM   LUNCH

2:00 PM   *Workshop Facilitator:*
             Introduction to Point 2 of Design Document:

             Audience Profiles
             SMALL GROUPS
             Small groups work on profiles of the project's intended audiences
             Share profiles with whole group

3:30 PM   TEA BREAK

4:00 PM   PLENARY
             Program Manager:
             Introduction to Point 3: Justification for chosen medium: Discussion on
             pros and cons of medium

5:30 PM   CLOSE

Day 2

8:00 AM   PLENARY
             Review of previous day (by designated participants)

Workshop Facilitator:
Point 4 of Document: Measurable Objectives of Serial as a whole. Presentation and discussion of overall objectives
Point 5 of Document: Presentation and discussion of overall purposes of Serial as a whole

10:30 AM	TEA BREAK
11:00 AM	Small Group Work

Point 6: Overall Message and Underlying Emotion(s)
Discussion of proposed overall message, and determination of appropriate emotion(s)

12:00 NOON	PLENARY

Workshop Facilitator:
Points 7 and 8: Number of programs and length (and format) of programs
Introduction to Points 9 and 10: Message Scope and Sequence
Small Group Work

1:00 PM	LUNCH
2:00 PM	PLENARY

Continuation and finalization of points 9 and 10
Review of all aspects of Design Document so far

3:30 PM	TEA BREAK
4:00 PM	PLENARY

Workshop Facilitator:
Part 2 of Design Document:
Introduction of how to determine specific message for each program
The Seven Cs of message preparation
Small group work on preparation of message for 1 program

5:30 PM	CLOSE

Day 3

8:00 AM	PLENARY

Review of previous day by selected participants
Presentation and discussion of previous day's messages by each group

9:00 AM	*Workshop Facilitator:*

Glossary introduction
Small group work continues on messages for specific programs

10:30 AM	TEA BREAK
11:00 AM	Small group work continues
1:00 PM	LUNCH
2:00 PM	Small group work continues

3:30 PM	TEA BREAK
4:00 PM	Small group work continues
5:30 PM	CLOSE

Day 4

8:00 AM	Review of previous day by selected participants
9:00 AM	Continuation of small group work
10:30 AM	TEA BREAK
11:00 AM	Completion of all small group work Sharing and reviewing messages (if time permits)
1:00 PM	LUNCH
2:00 PM	Glossary finalization (plenary)
3:30 PM	TEA BREAK
4:00 PM	Continuation of reviewing of all messages (if time allows) Writers work on preparation of story outlines
5:30 PM	CLOSE

Day 5

8:00 AM	Overview of entire workshop by designated participants
9:00 AM	Discussion of possible support materials (Listeners' guides, prizes, etc.)
10:30 AM	TEA BREAK
11:00 AM	Determination of all timelines, etc. Completion of all incomplete items
1:00 PM	LUNCH
2:00 PM	Presentation of story ideas by writers Written evaluations by team members
3:30 PM	TEA BREAK
4:00 PM	Finalization of all details
5:30 PM	CONCLUSION

Implementing the Agenda

The program manager will be the person responsible for ensuring a smooth-running workshop. Whether the agenda followed is the one suggested here or a slightly different one, it is helpful for the program manager to ensure that the various points discussed in this chapter are covered during the workshop.

Day 1

During the first working morning, the main facilitator can

- explain the purpose and objectives of the workshop.
- call for volunteers to be the first "daily reporters". Two reporters can be selected each day to prepare a summary of the day's achievements for presentation to the plenary group the following morning. This reporting helps the facilitators ensure that each day's activities are clearly understood by the team, and provides an opportunity for a question and discussion session at the start of each day.
- give a brief overview of the nature of Entertainment–Education programming and perhaps share a brief example of a television or film project using this format.
- explain the role and value of the design team and the importance of all members of the team being present throughout the whole workshop.
- explain the importance of the design document as the reliable reference for all message content and guide the team members briefly through the 7Cs of message content (see page 67).
- explain that most of the message creation will be done in small group work. If there are several different messages to be covered, each small group will deal with determining the precise messages for one topic. Where there are only one or two main topics, each small group will concentrate on one specific aspect of the topic.

The make-up of the groups should be decided in advance by the project staff. Each group should contain a similar mix of team members; for example: content specialist, audience representative, project staff member, other NGO members, ministry representative. The writers and director might like to move from group to group in order to gain a better understanding of the various topics being covered. Groups usually work more harmoniously together if they are limited to five members and if a group leader is appointed to guide the discussion. The following tips can help facilitate smooth group work.

- Draw attention to the listing of group members that should be posted in the workshop room, so members will know which group to join.
- If the design process is new to team members, it is helpful to have on hand copies of a design document from a previous project. Samples of design document pages are included in Appendix B of this book and can be used as a guide for team members.
- Share with the workshop participants the contents list of the design document either with printed copies of the contents list or with a Power Point or overhead presentation or both. (A sample copy of the Design Document Contents List appears on the following page.)

THE DESIGN DOCUMENT: CONTENTS

Part 1: Background and Overall Description

1. Justification (or rationale) for and statement of the desired change in behavior that the project wishes to encourage in the chosen audience
2. Information about the chosen audience(s)
3. Justification of the chosen medium or media*
4. The overall measurable objective(s) of the drama
5. The overall purpose(s) of the drama
6. Summary of the overall message and the main emotional focus of the message
7. The number of episodes to be created
8. The duration of each episode
9. The message scope and sequence (order in which message content must be given)
10. The number of episodes to be devoted to each topic (if more than one is needed)

Part 2: Individual Programs or Episodes

(For TV series or serial containing more than one episode)

11. The measurable objectives of each individual episode
12. The purpose of each individual episode
13. The precise message content of each episode
14. A glossary of topic-specific words and terms, together with the definitions (and translations) to be used in the scripts. An acronym list should also be included

Part 3: Implementation

15. Nomination of members of the script review team and the script support team
16. List and description of proposed support materials
17. Promotion plans and prizes or other incentives that will be provided to encourage the audience to listen and to act
18. The monitoring and evaluation plan

---

*Some behavior change campaigns use more than one medium: perhaps television and radio, or television and pri'

19. The time lines for

- all phases of script writing, reviewing, filming, editing, and broadcasting
- all phases of support and promotional material writing and dissemination
- all phases of evaluation:
  - pilot testing of scripts, support materials, and promotional materials
  - ongoing monitoring
  - summative evaluation
  - on air presentation

20. Story synopsis and sample program or episode

The finished design document might also include a responsibility list (or job description) for each person on the project team. Clear job descriptions help to avoid confusion over chain of command and individual responsibilities. The document usually also includes the names of all those who contributed to its successful completion.

Work on the Design Document

Once the workshop participants understand the objectives of the workshop and the meaning and importance of the design document, work on the document can be initiated on Day 1 itself.

1. Justification for the Project

The first item in the document—the **Justification** for the project—should be presented by one of the researchers who worked on the initial analysis of the problem and its causes. This presentation should be brief, clear, and to the point. It does not require all details of the research findings. Rather, a summary is required, outlining the problem, the audience affected by the problem, the apparent causes of the problem, the solutions that can be recommended, role-modeled and motivated through an Entertainment–Education drama, and perhaps a suggestion of the most appropriate behavior change theory to employ in the project. The presentation should take no more than half an hour and time should then be allowed for workshop participants to discuss the findings and ask questions as needed. Copies of the presentation should be made available for participants to refer to during small group activities.

Following the presentation of the research findings, the presenter might like to lead the group in a brief discussion of behavior change theories that might be applicable in this project.

Behavior change theories

Entertainment–Education dramas are developed to encourage people to adopt a new form of behavior—not just as individuals, but as a society. The greater aim of the drama is to have a positive effect on social norms, so that the recommended behavior change will become standard, accepted behavior for the entire community. Bringing about such change is not easy, and message developers, writers, and directors can benefit from some knowledge of the major theories that can most affect behavior change. A brief overview of some of these theories can help all team members determine the best way to focus their messages and assist the writers to develop their stories to effect positive social change. Some of the most useful behavior change theories include:

Diffusion theory

Theory developer: Everett Rogers

Basic tenet: Social networks and interpersonal communication are the major means of diffusing or spreading information and behavior change, and determining whether or not people will accept it. The diffusion theory suggests that as more and more people understand and practice a new behavior, it is more and more likely to become a social norm. Diffusion theory states that people measure a new behavior by considering its

- Comparative advantage: Does it give them any advantage over previous behavior?
- Compatibility: Does it fit in with their current beliefs and behaviors?
- Complexity: Is it difficult or relatively easy to adopt?
- Observability: Is it possible to observe what happens to others who adopt the new behavior?
- Trialability: Can they "try out" the new behavior safely before making a commitment to it?

Persuasion theory

Theory developer: W.J. McGuire

Basic tenet: Psychological factors play a significant role in determining a person's willingness to adopt a new behavior. These factors include:

- Personal attitude towards social issues and behavior
- Beliefs and concerns about the possible consequences of the new behavior
- Personal knowledge and skill in adapting to the new behavior
- Predispositions and preferences related to the behavior
- Beliefs or attitudes about the source of the teaching relative to the new behavior

The emphasis on **source** is of particular importance in persuasion theory, and this is especially pertinent to social development drama. If the persuasion theory is to be used, the design team and the writers must take into account the source(s) of information that audience members are most likely to trust. In some situations, this will be health personnel; in others it might be community leaders or religious leaders or educators. In some cases, the source that is most likely to appeal to the audience might well be a family member, or an admired older member of the community. In using this theory, the writer should also give serious consideration to the factors that affect persuasion and be sure they are correctly expressed in the drama.

Reasoned action theory

Theory developers: I. Ajzen and M. Fishbein

Basic tenet: People's willingness to adopt a new behavior is largely influenced by their beliefs about the possible consequences of the behavior, and their understanding of what the current social norms are with regard to this behavior. In other words, they like to reason their way through to an acceptance or rejection of a given behavior.

The theory of reasoned action emphasizes that people are often under stress while trying to make personal decisions as they consider, and reconsider, the possible consequences of their decisions. They can also be concerned about social pressure that seemingly might be trying to make them adopt behavior for which they are not yet quite ready.

Reasoned action is often the core of a good story or drama, as a character tries to make a decision on whether to move in one life direction or another.

Social learning theory

Theory developer: Albert Bandura

Basic tenet: People's willingness to adopt a new behavior is influenced by the overall social climate rather than by individual choice. According to the social learning theory, while considering a change in behavior, people

- observe what others are doing.
- consider the consequences of this new behavior in the lives of other people.
- contemplate what might happen in their own lives if they follow what others are doing.
- try out the new behavior for themselves.
- compare the results of the new behavior in their own lives with how it has affected others. If the results are pleasing, they confirm their belief in the new behavior and adopt it.

This social learning approach to behavior change is very common in many forms of literature, including drama. It is not at all uncommon for characters in a drama (as in real life) to be influenced by someone else's behavior and wish to be like that person. As they begin to follow in the footsteps of their role model, they gradually gain a sense of self-efficacy and become more and more confident that the new behavior is right for them.

It is beneficial if the research team can make some recommendation as to which behavior change theory is most likely to be effective in the current project. If this information is not provided, however, the design team (including the writers and the director) can discuss and determine which behavior change theory might be most appropriate in their current project.

2. The Audience

The next step of the document can be carried out in small groups. If there is more than one audience to be reached, each group can concentrate on a separate audience. Otherwise each group should put together its own analysis of the audience and then discuss the findings in a plenary session.

In order to bring about successful behavior change, many things need to be understood about each intended audience, including the following:

- age
- educational level and literacy level
- social standing
- attitude to the behavior that should be changed
- reasons for current attitude
- current interest or lack thereof in changing behavior
- possible motivators of change (change agents)
- possible obstacles to behavior change
- viewing habits
- types of programs enjoyed by the audience
- family "program selector"—the person in the family who determines what programs the family members will watch. If the program format or the drama story has no appeal for the family program selector (often a male), it is likely that it will not be watched.

The compilation of this information is absolutely necessary in order for the messages to be expressed and presented in an appropriate manner, and for the characters and action of the drama to attract and hold the attention of the audience(s). Participants should be encouraged to keep the audience profiles in mind as they determine what messages will be included in the drama and how they should be expressed.

Causes and change agents (motivators)

Of paramount importance to those working on a behavior change project is a clear understanding of the **cause(s)** of the audience's current behavior. Without the knowledge of why people are behaving the way they are, it is virtually impossible to know how to encourage them to change. If the current behavior is based on traditional, cultural or religious beliefs, it will be much harder to change than if it results from a simple lack of knowledge. Similarly, change that refers to prevention rather than cure (e.g., preventing injury by wearing a seat belt in the car) is often very difficult to motivate.

Similarly valuable is the determination of the **change agents** or **motivators** that are most likely to encourage the chosen audience to alter their behavior. Change agents can be people, emotions, actions, events or benefits. With adolescents, for example, it is almost universally true that the most effective motivators are their peers. Most adolescents like to be seen as part of the "in group"; they do not like to be seen as different from or standing apart from others their own age. Consequently, a film made to bring about behavior change in an adolescent audience is more likely to be successful if the desired changes are modeled by other adolescents than if they are dictated by adult mentors. Older people in small rural villages may be influenced by characters portraying traditional authority figures such as tribal elders and chiefs. Powerful change agents for urban and suburban viewers might be the opportunity to become richer or more influential. In situations dealing with topics like family planning, the most convincing change agents might be different for men than they are for women. For women, the chance to be pregnant less often, to have more leisure time and to pursue personal interests can be powerful persuaders. Men, on the other hand, might be more easily persuaded to have small families if they are convinced this will increase their financial well-being and their acceptance as "modern" males or if they believe that their wives will stay beautiful longer if they have fewer children.

Understanding the nature of the change agents or motivators that are likely to work for a particular audience is an essential first step in determining the storyline and the characters for the film project. The audience representatives in the design team can contribute helpful knowledge about possible change agents and influential community members. Writers can include in the drama fictional role models based on these people.

It is only with a very clear understanding of the chosen audience that the design team can make effective decisions on all the other components of the design document. Knowing the audience well will help ensure that the message content is stated in a way that is meaningful to them.

For example: In some countries the term "Family Planning" is considered unacceptable; the term "child spacing" is much more acceptable. Similarly, in some countries the term "Adolescent Reproductive Health" is disallowed because it seems to suggest inappropriate behavior for adolescents. More acceptable is the term "Adolescent Physical and Mental Health" or even the more general term "Adolescent Life." The often used ABC for HIV prevention (Abstain; Be faithful; use a Condom) is not acceptable to many religious organizations, who much prefer an ABC that stands for Accept responsibility; Be prepared; Consider the consequences.

3. Justification for the Chosen Medium

Point 3 of the document can be discussed in the plenary session: the Justification for the Chosen Medium. Every medium has advantages and disadvantages and it is valuable for both message designers and drama writers to be aware of these. It is easy to overlook the fact that there are disadvantages with visual media, just as there are with radio or print. The major disadvantage of film or television is that very little is left to the imagination of the audience. Where radio and print allow audience members to visualize characters and settings to suit their own liking, film and television make those decisions for them. Appearances that appeal to one ethnic group in a community might be totally uninteresting or unacceptable to others. The design team needs to carefully consider the advantages and limitations of the chosen medium so that these can be kept in mind as messages and stories are developed.

In considering the justification for the use of television, the design team also might have to make decisions on such matters as location and actors. It can be valuable for a decision to be made at this stage on the area or region of the country in which the film should be shot, so that writers can take this into account during scripting. Before the creative work of writing and filming commences, the writer and the director need to know if the chosen audience is specifically rural or specifically urban or if the message pertains more to people in one part of a country than others. Similarly, if there is a feeling that certain famous actors should be employed for the sake of attracting the audience, the design team and the director should discuss this. It should be remembered that while famous artists might be a way of attracting an audience, they can also be a distraction from the message. Dramas designed for social change should reflect, as much as possible, real life and real people. Sometimes, previously unknown artists can be more convincing as representatives of real life.

Using drama

Following the discussion of the advantages and challenges of the chosen medium, the plenary group might like to discuss the type of program being planned: drama—especially serial drama—and consider why this is likely to be appropriate for the project needs (see Chapter 1).

At the end of the first day, the facilitator can briefly recap the first day's accomplishments and encourage participants to be ready to contribute to the next day's activities.

Day 2

Each morning can begin with the day's reporters giving an overview of the previous day's accomplishments. Their report should be kept very brief, giving a simple outline of what was achieved the previous day. Participants should then be encouraged to ask questions or give comments, so that the achievements of the first day are agreed upon before the design work continues. Work can then begin on Point 4 of the design document: measurable objectives.

4. Measurable Objectives of the Project as a Whole

Measurable objectives apply to the audience: what the project plans to achieve with the audience in terms of knowledge gain, attitude development and action taken. The overall measurable objectives must be realistic, but clearly in line with the aims of the project. *For example*, one objective might be:

> *As a result of this serial drama, there will be a measurable increase in the number of young couples who seek family planning counseling together.*

This objective is measurable (perhaps by gathering information from health providers before and after the drama is broadcast); it is also realistic in that it is not demanding impossible changes, such as *"all young couples will come together to seek family planning counseling."*

Determining the overall measurable objectives for the Entertainment–Education intervention can be done by the design team as a whole. This is time-consuming, however, and can lead to lengthy discussion of minor points. Generally, it is preferable for the facilitator or the researcher to present to the team suggested overall measurable objectives that were determined by the research team, based on their findings. These can then be discussed by the team, and altered as necessary.

If the drama serial is dealing with several different topics, there should be only one, or at the most two overall objectives for each topic. These objectives can be broken down into more specific terms when individual program design is carried out.

5. Overall Purposes of the Project as a Whole

The clarification of the "purpose" of the project provides guidelines for the message designers, the writer(s) and the director. The "purpose" explains what approach the project as a whole must take in order to encourage behavior change.

For example, if the topic is completely **new** to the audience, it will be necessary for the drama to "educate" or "provide specific knowledge to" the audience. This specific knowledge must be clearly spelled out in the messages, and the drama must include actions or events that allow for a natural but accurate dissemination of the knowledge. If the behavior change is one about which the audience is very well informed, but still resists, the message creators and the writers will need to be aware that the main purpose of the drama is **to motivate** acceptance and practice of the behavior change. In dealing with the topic of HIV and AIDS, for example, the purpose or approach of the drama would be very different if dealing with an audience that knows nothing about how the disease is spread, than dealing with an audience that knows the facts but resists appropriate protection behavior. Usually, the overall purposes of an Entertainment–Education project will be two, three, or perhaps four of the following:

- to educate
- to reinforce (or update) knowledge
- to stimulate interest in behavior change
- to model appropriate behavior change
- to provide information on resources
- to motivate behavior change
- to encourage sharing of information and behavior change in order to establish new social norms
- to demonstrate how to do something associated with the behavior change, such as counseling couples on adopting family planning.

6. Overall Message Summary

One of the major challenges facing the design team is to keep messages simple and concise. The natural tendency is to want to give the audience every bit of available information on the topic. Too much knowledge, however, is as bad as too little. An over-abundance of knowledge cannot be absorbed and is likely to turn the audience away. One way to help avoid knowledge overkill is by obtaining team agreement on a brief overall summary of the messages. The summary should be a simple, one paragraph statement of the most motivating message for the audience.

For example:

> The most important protection from HIV and AIDS is **personal responsibility**. The HIV and AIDS pandemic can be overcome only if every person (particularly every man) from this day forward accepts **personal responsibility** for knowing the details of how the disease is spread, and always (without exception) protecting himself/herself from infection and for ensuring that he/she never puts another person at risk of infection.

This message summary is blunt and brief. At the same time, it helps the message designers and the creative artists to know exactly where the emphasis of the messages will be. The message summary can be prepared in advance of the workshop and shared with the design team for their comment and approval.

Main emotion
Entertainment–Education combines the emotional power of a good story with the intellectual strength of important knowledge. To assist the writer(s) in making the story

appropriately powerful, it is helpful for the team to consider what emotion is most likely to motivate the audience to want to adopt a change of behavior. Perhaps fear is a likely motivator, or hope, or pride, or love. Perhaps it will require a combination of two or more emotions to guide the audience in the right direction. The determination of the appropriate emotion(s) which should underlie the story rests on a thorough knowledge and understanding of the audience(s) and the reasons for their current behavior or resistance to change.

7. Number of Programs

It is tempting to think that the more programs there are, the greater will be the chance of effecting behavior change. This is not necessarily true. One really powerful drama can shock people into seeing their own lives in a different light and making an immediate change, just as the movie *On The Beach* (1959) scared the world into the realization of just what atomic fallout could do to the entire planet. However, it is certainly true that when people are asked to make a lifestyle change that might not seem to them immediately necessary or possible, it is helpful for the change to be presented to them gradually but consistently over time. One of the great advantages of the drama serial is that it can portray a character (or characters) who start out reluctant to change and who move gradually and comfortably in the new direction.

   The determination of how many episodes will be in a TV drama serial will depend on several things including budget, but there is general agreement in the Entertainment–Education world that the minimum number of programs should be 26 (that is, six months at the rate of one episode a week). If the same episode can be shown more than once—at different times during the week—this can be helpful. It should be remembered also that the quality of the drama serial is equally important. A poorly balanced and constructed Entertainment–Education drama that runs for several years can be less effective than one that is very well designed and written and runs for only six months.

8. Length of the Program

The determination of how long each drama program or serial episode should be largely depends on the following:

- the broadcast station's usual program length
- the program length to which the audience is accustomed
- the cost of air time
- the quality of the production

The audience will quickly lose interest and stop watching if the drama is poorly written or produced and goes on for too long. At the same time, the allotted time should be sufficient to allow the messages to come in naturally and comfortably. For an Entertainment–Education drama serial, there is general agreement that each episode should be at least 30 minutes and not more than 60 minutes.

9. & 10. Message Scope and Sequence

Determining the scope and sequence of the messages in a social development drama serial is very similar to determining the curriculum and lesson plans for an educational course or the chapters in a text book. Good teachers know where to start each lesson; when to move forward to a new topic; which topics are likely to be most difficult for their students to understand and/or to practice; which topics are likely to have to be repeated in order for the students to really grasp their meaning and importance. Similarly, in determining the scope and sequence of the messages for a social development drama serial, the design team must take into account: (a) the audience's current knowledge; (b) their willingness and ability to change; and (c) their ability to absorb, understand and practice the desired behavior change. The "lesson plan" or scope and sequence of the messages will be guided by this knowledge.

The design team will determine exactly what topics will be covered and the order in which they should be included in the serial. Consider a drama that aims to help people protect themselves from infectious diseases such as Avian 'flu or Sudden Acute Respiratory Syndrome (SARS). The design team will have to decide the precise facts the audience will need and the order in which they should receive the facts. Should the opening message be a shock: how easily death can result from these diseases? Or should the early messages be about symptoms, or about causes, or about preventive behavior, or a combination of these topics? The team must also determine what behavior change motivators to include and whether to put factual knowledge and behavior change motivation together in each episode or to present them separately.

When the Entertainment–Education drama serial is designed to deal with a wider variety of topics (such as family health), the team has even more complicated decisions to make. They must determine the order in which the topics will be presented; whether all programs on the same topic will be grouped together or spread throughout the drama episodes; and how many episodes will be devoted to each aspect of the main topic.

Often, the research team can provide helpful guidelines in determining topic scope and sequence. Their findings can indicate where the biggest problems lie, where the most resistance to change occurs or what knowledge the audience needs most. The main topics can be written on cards and pinned on a board as is done in the Visualization in Participatory Planning (VIPP) method.* The design team can then discuss the nature

---

*The first manual for VIPP, targeted at facilitators and trainers involved in participatory group events, was written by Neill McKee, Herman Tillmann, and Maria Angelica Salas. It was published by UNICEF Bangladesh in 1993.

and order of the subtopics and pin these in place as they are determined. The use of the card system makes it quick and easy to change the subtopics and the order of their presentation until final agreement is reached.

Once the topics have been determined and arranged in order, the design team groups are ready to work on the precise message content for the individual episodes. This can usually begin on the afternoon of the second day.

Individual Episode Messages

Keeping in mind the necessity of suiting the messages to the audience, the facilitator should remind design team members at this stage of the workshop of the importance of ensuring that the message content as recorded in the design document is correct, complete, clear, concise, consistent, culturally appropriate and compelling (see Box 3.1).

Correct messages

Every detail of the message presented to the audience must be **correct**. If audience members learn at some point that even a small detail of the messages has been exaggerated or is not entirely true, they will lose trust in the program and lose interest in the recommended behavior change. For example, a message that states that "children who are given a proper diet *will be* mentally brighter" is not necessarily true in every case. It would be better to say, "Children who are given a proper diet will have a better chance of being mentally brighter." Where advertising sometimes "manipulates" its messages to attract and influence the audience, entertainment–education dramas must ensure that their messages are always 100 per cent accurate and correct.

Complete messages

As the drama is prepared, decisions must be made on exactly how much information relating to a particular message or part of a message will go into each episode. This means there must be careful selection of the message content, so that the message within each program is complete. A program or episode that tells the audience about the importance of protecting themselves from HIV/AIDS and then adds that information on protection will be given in another program is incomplete and therefore dangerous. By the time the next program comes around, someone in the audience may already—in the meantime—have indulged in behavior that will result in contracting the disease. The message content should include, at the very least, the information that advice about protection from HIV/AIDS can be obtained at hospitals and health posts. Then, it is safe to add that more information on protection from HIV/AIDS will be given in the next program. While it is obvious that not every program can give all the information on a particular topic, there should be assurance that the audience is at least told where to go for immediate help and further information.

Clear and logical messages

Content specialists are very important members of the design team. Frequently, however, these specialists are accustomed to discussing topics in professional or scientific language, which might not be appropriate to or easily understood by the audience. Audience representatives on the team can help ensure that the words used are understandable. Writers, also, should question any technical words or language used by content specialists, and ask for clear explanations so that they will know how to pass on the information to their viewers. The **Glossary** included in the design document is used to list the simple, clear definitions of technical language that the writer should use in the scripts. Initials and acronyms commonly used by content specialists and others (such as ministry representatives) are frequently not known to the audience and should be avoided. For this reason an Acronym List is included with the Glossary to provide the writer with the full meaning of each acronym.

Box 3.1

The 7 Cs of Message Presentation

Messages in Entertainment–Education dramas must be

Correct
Complete
Clear and Logical
Concise
Consistent
Culturally appropriate
Compelling

Logical Messages: Information that seems sensible and perfectly logical to content specialists sometimes makes little sense to an audience.

For example, recommending that a "balanced diet" is necessary for a child's growth might seem perfectly sensible to a nutritionist, but what does "balanced diet" mean to the average member of a rural community? In a case like this, the message can be made logical be giving examples of the types and amounts of foods that are required for proper growth. Design team members must ensure that every message makes complete and logical sense to their audience members.

Concise messages

At the same time, it is necessary to make sure that the messages are concise, and therefore easy to recall. In a drama episode lasting 20–30 minutes, the actual spoken message details should occupy no more than 5–8 minutes, at the most. This means that there can be no lengthy lecture on the message given at any time. The message details must be worked in naturally and concisely. Team members need to think through carefully what is the *very least* that can be said to encourage appropriate behavior change.

For example, in a drama designed to encourage the general public to plan and space their families by using contraceptives, it is not necessary to provide every detail of every available contraceptive. The important facts are that it is possible to space the birth of children by using modern contraceptives; that there are several types of contraceptives available—all of which have been found to be safe—and that couples should visit their local clinic or health provider for information and counseling on the various contraceptives, together with help on determining which one would be right for them. It is usually impossible for viewers to recall specific details of such things as contraceptive methods from what they hear in a half-hour drama episode, so it is important for design team members to determine how to give the most important details in a concise and clear manner.

Consistent messages

One lesson that message designers can learn from advertisers is the importance of message consistency. Advertisers make regular and repeated use of slogans and catch phrases that encourage customers to recall their product. Similarly, those who are creating social change messages should always remember the importance of making their messages **consistent**. It is on the matter of consistency that the "magazine" or "variety program" format is not recommended for behavior change programs. The use of different guest speakers or testimonials each week makes it difficult to ensure that the different speakers will present the important messages in a consistent manner. Consistency is a vital stimulant of memory. Audiences are far more likely to recall and act upon suggested behaviors if the main points of the recommended behavior are always expressed in the same words. For example, one Asian drama always referred to the practice of giving dowry as "an unnecessary, illegal threat to a happy marriage." No matter which character in the story discussed dowry, these same words were used in the discussion. It is much easier for an audience to recall important points if they are consistently expressed.

Culturally appropriate messages

Cultural appropriateness is of particular importance in programs created for the visual media. Of equal importance with the wording of the message is the visual presentation of such items as clothing, living conditions, and location. All these must be representative of and acceptable to the audience for whom the message is designed. Absolute accuracy and precision is vital to every part of every message contained in the design document. (The sample design document in Appendix B demonstrates the precision with which the messages must be selected and worded.) Similarly, the choice of character to deliver the messages is equally important; this character must be someone the audience trusts.

Compelling messages

Behavior change messages are inevitably based on fact. It is a fact that people who regularly smoke cigarettes have a 1 in 2 chance of dying as a result of their habit. This fact alone, however, is usually not enough to encourage people to quit smoking. One real advantage of using drama to deliver behavior change messages is that the facts can be made more compelling by demonstrating them in the lives of characters who are important to or loved by the audience. The design document provides the important facts that the audience needs; the writer and director create the compelling emotional environment in which these facts can be made personal and powerful to the audience. The writer(s) will be guided by the emotional emphasis that was determined for Point 6 of the design document.

"Committed": This is another word that can be added to the checklist for message content. Those creating the messages should consider whether this behavior change is something to which the audience can feel and remain committed. In other words, is it something which they feel has truly become part of their normal way of living?

To close out Day 2, each small group should be invited to work on the message design for one episode on their list of topics, and be prepared to share it with other team members the following day. Sharing these first efforts helps all team members to understand where the difficulties in message design lie and how they can be overcome.

Day 3 and day 4

After the presentation of the daily report on Day 3, the facilitator can remind team members of the purpose and importance of the glossary. Technical terms and acronyms that are commonplace to topic specialists are usually not understood by the general public, or even by the writers.

The Glossary

The aim of the glossary is to provide simple, clear, appropriate definitions of technical words and phrases that can be used comfortably by the writers and be easily understood by all audience members. Writers and directors should question anything in the messages that does not make clear and comfortable sense to them, bearing in mind that it is their job to ensure absolute understanding on the part of the audience. If the design document is being prepared in one language (perhaps English), but the scripts are to be created in another, it is vital that the glossary includes the local language translation of difficult terms.

Some facilitators like to appoint two or three people to be in charge of the glossary; to accept and revise all glossary entries from team members and put them in an alphabetical list to share with the full team—for review and possible revision—before the end of the workshop.

Days 3 and 4 of the design workshop are devoted primarily to the completion of the message content for the individual episodes. This work might well continue through

Day 5 if the number of team members is limited, or if there are more than 26 episodes to be designed.

The Writer's Work Begins

By Day 4 of the workshop, the writer(s) and director(s) should have a good sense of what they are going to be required to do. It can be valuable to dismiss the "creative" members from the team in the middle of Day 4, inviting each of them to start preparing a brief story synopsis to present to the design team before the end of the workshop.

Reviewing the Message Content Pages

Whether or not every episode message is presented for review by the entire design team depends to a large degree on the number of episodes to be prepared and the time available at the workshop. Often it is preferable to put the message pages into the hands of a competent editor who can then prepare them for review. A short review workshop (1 or 2 days) can be arranged shortly after the design workshop, attended by a select number of design team members (the review team). The work of this review team will be essentially to ensure that all messages adhere to the 7Cs of message presentation.

Day 5 and day 6

In the plenary session, the design team members can review the glossary and make a joint decision as to which suggested entries are needed and if all are correct.

On the day before the end of the workshop, the writers can present an outline of the stories they have in mind. Workshop participants can be invited to give a *written assessment* of the writers' presentations (see Script Evaluation Sheet in Appendix A). Inviting open discussion on the writers' ideas tends to be less than helpful. Team members almost always have their own ideas on what the story should be about or who the characters should be. Trying to discuss and coordinate a wide variety of ideas can lead to confusion. Team members who have specific ideas for a storyline or characters can be invited to present them briefly on the back of the evaluation form.

Final day(s) of the design workshop

Once the episode message content pages have been completed, the remaining work (Part 3) of the Design Document can be undertaken: **Implementation**. Such considerations as the make up of the Script Support Team (two or three people who will be readily available to answer message questions that might occur while the writers are scripting) can be determined by the program manager alone. Similarly, the program manager can determine the script review team, making sure that those selected for this team will be available throughout the script writing phase. It should be noted that reviewing or editing every script is essential. It is easy for even the best writers to make small, inadvertent errors that can mislead or misinform the audience, either with regard to the story or the message. Every successful writer in the world (drama, fiction, poetry, etc.) has at least one editor to ensure that everything is correct before publication. In the case of behavior change drama, script review and editing is even more vital because the health and lives of people are at stake.

The members of the design team should be involved in decisions relating to such areas as Support Materials, Promotion and most particularly—the Time Line. Moving a project from the design workshop stage to being on air is a challenging task and it is advantageous for all participants to have an understanding of what is required to enable the project to move forward smoothly. The director and the writers should be present during the discussion and determination of the timelines. Their contribution at this stage is very important.

AFTER THE DESIGN WORKSHOP

By the end of the design workshop, the team will have put together a first draft of the design document, which will be sufficiently accurate to be used by the writers as they prepare their audition synopsis/treatment of the story. While the writers are working, the draft document should be checked by the review team for accuracy and completeness.

The program manager can call together the review team as soon as possible after the design workshop to review and, where necessary, revise the draft of the design document. The approved and finalized document will be distributed to all appropriate people, including the writer and the director who will use the document as their reliable reference for all stages of program development. Some projects like to have a signatory page at the beginning of the document on which to record signatures of approval from project leaders and others whose approval is vital to the success of the project.

Preparing the Story Synopsis

While the design document is being reviewed and revised as needed, the writer prepares a brief story synopsis (treatment) and character profiles of **all plots** (typically a 26- or 52-part serial will have one main plot and three or four subplots), together with one complete audition script (if one is required).

The Finished Synopsis

The finished synopsis should show a blend of the following elements that are essential for successful Entertainment–Education visual drama:

- a story type that appeals to the chosen audience
- a main plot and subplots that allow the natural, gradual and subtle blending in of the necessary educational message(s) and behavior change modeling determined by the design team
- strong visual highlights to move the story along
- adherence to the ten principles of story development (see Chapter 4)
- characters whose personalities contribute naturally to the jeopardy or conflict in the story and to its eventual resolution
- characters who can explain, model or demonstrate the desired behavior change

Synopsis Sample

The following sample is from the famous Indian series *Jasoos Vijay* and shows how the story is briefly outlined in this initial synopsis. At the same time, even this brief outline shows how the messages will be woven into the story:

Episode 1 entitled *'Missing Bride'* has Jasoos Vijay going to a village in Rajasthan to investigate the family background of a potential bride (Tara). However, on reaching the village, Vijay discovers that Tara has been missing for the past couple of days. While delving into this issue, he comes across her dead body thrown into an abandoned well. As the mystery unfolds, Vijay reaches the conclusion that it was Tara's cousin, Deepak, who had killed her. A sympathetic and sensitive Tara used to meet an HIV-positive person, Pratap, who was forced to leave the village because of the negative attitude of the community towards him. Deepak's fear was that by merely visiting Pratap, Tara could have been infected with the virus, and thereafter transmit it to the entire village. This fear drove him to murder Tara.

The messages in this storyline focus on facts of AIDS, routes of transmission, care and support for people living with HIV/AIDS (PLWHA) and myths and misconceptions related to AIDS. Certain gender-based messages related to domestic violence are also included in this story.

Episode 2, 'Kidnapped': Jasoos Vijay solves a case of a major robbery in a jeweler's shop. In the midst of this case, Vijay and Gauri (who has become his able assistant) witness a young girl, Radha, being chased by some men on the road. Unfortunately, before they can rescue her, they lose track of the group. On the following day, Vijay sees Radha running out of the jewelry shop of his client (Seth Deena Nathji). On reaching there, Vijay finds his frail old client unconscious and wounded. He meets up with Radha's parents and learns from them about Kartik, the man to whom they married off Radha. Soon Vijay realizes that the latter had been a victim of circumstances as she was being forced into sex work but had been rescued by Vijay's client, Sethji. When Vijay rescues Radha, it is revealed that she is HIV positive. At first Radha's father does not accept his daughter back and expresses several misconceptions about HIV. Vijay explains to Radha's father the modes of transmission. The story ends with Radha being accepted by her family and being able to lead a fulfilling life while taken appropriate medications and care. Her story provides a positive message in support of PLWHA.

For the HIV/AIDS messages, the focus is on the facts, myths and misconceptions of HIV/AIDS, routes of transmission, dual benefits of condoms, correct use of condoms and care and support for PLWHA.

A similar brief synopsis was presented for each episode in the series.

Reviewing the Synopsis

Once the synopsis is complete, it will be read by the review team before the writer begins full scripting. If the review team recommends any changes, these will be discussed fully with the writer(s) and decisions should be made jointly about which of the changes to incorporate. When the review team is satisfied with the story, the characters and the method of message inclusion, the writer can go ahead with writing the individual scripts.

Review Guidelines

The program manager can share the following review guidelines with the review team to help ensure that everyone is reviewing the same things in the same way. Review team members should look for the following points in each plot to determine whether it is culturally appropriate, likely to hold the attention of the audience and equally likely to be able to accommodate the message content, and result in a successful Entertainment–Education drama:

1. What is the central dramatic conflict in the plot?
2. What is the predominant emotion of the plot?
3. Will the central conflict and the predominant emotion appeal to the chosen audience?
4. Does the plot open with some action or question that will grab the viewer's attention?

5. How many characters are in the plot? Are there too many, too few, a sufficient number?
6. Will the main characters appeal to the audience(s)?
7. Which of the message topics will be included in the plot?
8. Is it clear that this story has important VISUAL elements that make it suitable for presentation through television or film?
9. Are some of the main characters representative of the chosen audience?
10. Are the characters individual rather than stereotyped? Does each main character have a clear and distinct personality?
11. Are some characters included for whom it might be difficult or impossible to find appropriate actors? (Take particular note of the requirement for young child actors. These can be difficult to cast.)
12. Are there some main characters who demonstrate (or model) the benefits of the desired behavior change?
13. Are there some characters who are on the same step of the behavior change model as the majority of the chosen audience?
14. If the chosen audience likes music in drama, does at least one plot allow for the natural introduction of music: a musician as a character, perhaps?
15. If the audience is attracted to humor (and it is hard to find an audience that is not) is there a humorous character or a humorous incident in one of the plots? Remember that even a tragic story can include some humor if it is well handled.
16. Is it clear where and how each part of the message outlined in the design document will come into which plot or subplot?
17. Can the messages or parts of the message be introduced in the correct sequence, in accordance with the requirements of the design document?
18. Are there any scenes or locations that would be very difficult or impossible to include, such as an earthquake or a tidal wave? (While it is possible to use existing footage, known as "stock footage", from other sources for scenes like these, it is never entirely satisfactory because stock footage often has a second-hand look or a different color quality from the new film being shot.)
19. Does it seem that the drama will fit comfortably into the broadcast length that was decided upon during the design workshop?
20. Is the story interesting, original and believable (even though fictional)?

By the time the plot outlines have been written and reviewed, the final version of the design document should be completed. The selected writer is then given a copy of the document and asked to go ahead with the full plot synopsis of **all episodes**, making sure that the message content and sequence in the document is strictly maintained. A sample of a full story synopsis is contained in Chapter 4.

Writers should be encouraged to refer as needed to those design team members who have been selected as the **script support team**. In this way questions and difficulties can be answered as they arise rather than allowing the script to continue with errors or inconsistencies.

When the full synopsis of all episodes has been approved by the review team, the writer(s) can begin work on individual episodes. Each episode will be reviewed by the review team to ensure message accuracy and story attraction.

PART 3

For the
Writer

4

ARTISTRY
Writing Entertainment–Education Drama

Writing Entertainment–Education drama requires talent and dedication.

THE CHALLENGE OF ENTERTAINMENT–EDUCATION WRITING

Writing drama for Entertainment–Education films or television is a challenging task because it combines two skills that might seem quite different from each other. Entertainment is designed to arouse, and then engage, the emotions of the audience, while education is designed to impart precise, relevant knowledge and promote new behavior in specific audiences. The two can, however, be harmoniously blended together.

The writer has to create an enthralling story* that will appeal to the chosen audience(s) and will attract and hold their attention. Into that story the writer must blend the precise knowledge messages and behavior models that have been prescribed or determined by the design team to encourage a particular behavior change that can help in overcoming a current problem.

The difficulty, however, is that many of the behaviors that Entertainment–Education programs address are complex and not easily changed. Of particular difficulty are behaviors based in strong cultural tradition. The challenge is for the writer to encourage the audience to consider the recommended changes from an objective position, while at the same time being emotionally attracted to the story. Sometimes, the best the drama can do is to stimulate discussion of the desired change and its possible advantages and leave the audience to make their own decisions.

---

*The story is the sequence of events in which the characters are involved. A story can be presented in many forms: drama, narrative, dance, picture, etc.

It is helpful for writers to understand where the chosen audience currently stands on the Steps to Behavior Change (Box 4.1). With this knowledge, it is usually easier to create realistic, believable characters who start out on the same step as the audience. As the story develops, at least some of these characters can progress to the desired behavior change level. In their progression, they can demonstrate clearly how progression can be made and how the desired changes are relevant and beneficial to the viewing audience.

It is equally valuable for writers to give consideration to the behavior change theories that were introduced in Chapter 3 and perhaps discussed in the workshop, and consider which approach, suggested by these theories, would be most appropriate for the behavior they hope to change and the audience for whom they are writing.

The Entertainment–Education drama writer has a goal markedly different from that of a writer whose only objective is entertainment. The primary goal of Entertainment–Education drama writing is to motivate the audience to explore the possibilities of improving, perhaps even saving, their own lives and/or the lives of others. Entertainment–Education writers must gain the respect and trust of their audiences so that they believe the message facts that are presented.

Box 4.1

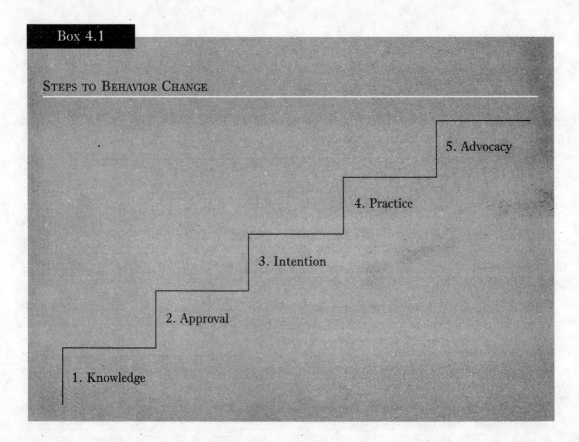

STEPS TO BEHAVIOR CHANGE

5. Advocacy

4. Practice

3. Intention

2. Approval

1. Knowledge

THE MESSAGE IS NOT THE STORY

Entertainment–Education drama writers should understand that the message is not the story. Even if the message is an important part of the story, there must be other action, other dilemmas, other conflicts in which the main characters are involved. A drama that centres solely on the message tends to become didactic and runs the risk of being boring. Audiences quickly realize when a drama is being used as a disguise for a lecture.

See, for example, the different approaches used in Boxes 4.2 and 4.3. The drama will be much more effective if the story exists in advance of the message.

Box 4.2

MESSAGE AS STORY

A young woman of 15 is pregnant for the first time. She is really too young to be pregnant but her husband has insisted they have a child.

The pregnancy runs into trouble and the young woman's life is threatened.

Will she live or will she die?

The main character in this story—the young woman—exists only to deliver the message about the dangers of early pregnancy.

Box 4.3

STORY WITH MESSAGE BLENDED IN

A young woman of 15 has a truly beautiful voice. Everyone loves to hear her sing. She has entered a national competition for the most beautiful voice in the land, and her singing teacher is confident that she can win. But her marriage has been arranged and her husband wants her to become pregnant right away. He loves to hear her sing and is very proud of her voice, but his family is pressing him to have a son.

The singing teacher begs the husband to let his wife wait until after the competition before starting a family. The husband is angry and tells the teacher to mind his own business. He says the teacher is only interested in making money by giving his wife lessons. He says he never wants to see the teacher again and tells his wife she can have no more singing lessons. Her job is to be a mother.

(Box 4.3 contd)

(Box 4.3 contd)

The singing teacher is afraid of the husband. Nevertheless, he comes to the husband very early one morning and begs him to listen as he reveals the real reason he wants the young woman to delay pregnancy. He relates the tragic story of his own wife who died in childbirth because she was too young when she became pregnant. The baby died as well, and the teacher does not want to see this happen to his student. He begs the husband to get advice from the doctor.

Will the husband go to the doctor for advice? Will he agree to delay pregnancy? Is it already too late; is the wife already pregnant? Will she resume her singing? Will she win the competition?

The characters in this story have a life beyond the message and yet the message is an integral part of the plot.

Similarly, as was indicated in the synopsis sample earlier in this book (pages 72–73), the Indian *Jasoos Vijay* series used the exciting story of a detective's life and the many mysteries it involves, as the medium through which to introduce valuable lessons on HIV and AIDS.

THE STRUCTURE OF DRAMA

Every successful story, whether narrative or dramatic, follows the structure shown in the Figure 4.1. Some writers (such as Hollywood dramatists) describe script structure of a film as three "acts", based on the structure of live drama in theaters.

Figure 4.1

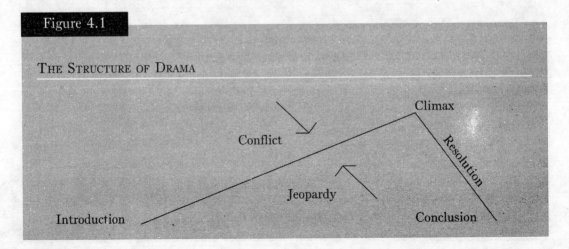

THE STRUCTURE OF DRAMA

The Introduction

The introduction of any drama

- establishes the main character or characters.
- reveals their environment and circumstances.
- demonstrates something of their personalities.
- sets up and establishes the conflict.
- starts the action so the audience can begin to guess how the personalities of the leading characters will react to the conflict. For example, a very shy person who witnesses a crime will try to run away and hide rather than be caught up in a glare of publicity. An egotistical person on the other hand, caught in the same predicament, will seek the limelight of the courtroom and the news cameras.
- hints at the underlying emotion or universal theme. For example, in the story involving a shy person witnessing a crime, the underlying emotion might be "bravery." This emotion would begin to become evident right at the beginning of the story as the shy person displays a lack of bravery, which later becomes her dominant characteristic. On the other hand, a story involving an egotistical person caught in the same predicament might have an underlying theme of "pride comes before a fall." The audience would be subtly aware of this right from the beginning of the drama, as the egotist's behavior reflects foolishness.

The Development

This is the major part of the story, and it

- moves the action forward.
- enhances dramatic conflict or jeopardy (see page 89) and puts the audience in a state of suspense wanting to know which way the conflict will be resolved. The action and the conflict mount throughout the development until it comes to the breaking point: the climax.

The Climax

This is that part of the story where "one side has to win." For example, the day of the court judgement has arrived. The shy woman realizes that an innocent person will be sent to jail for life if she does not speak up. There can be no more delay. She must speak up now and risk becoming a public figure, or shut up for ever and let an innocent person suffer. This is the climax: something MUST happen NOW.

The Resolution

This is the aftermath of the climax, that leads quickly to the conclusion. For example, the conflict is resolved when the shy person determines to tell the truth. She is offered witness protection so that she can keep her personal life private. The innocent person is freed.

The Conclusion

This comes swiftly after the resolution. Once the conflict has been resolved, the story concludes.

THE COMPONENTS OF DRAMA

Just as all good dramas have a common structure, they also have common components. These include:

Characters

The people (or perhaps animals—as in many legends) who are involved in the action and who have clear personality characteristics that contribute to the conflict.

Locations (settings)

Every story happens somewhere and at some time. The choice of locations is an important part of making the story realistic and relevant to the chosen audience. Ideally, Entertainment–Education dramas are set in present time so that they can be relevant to a present day audience who can see that the recommended behavior change can and should be adopted now.

Plot (action)

The events and conflicts in which the characters are involved. The action reveals how their personalities and the events in which they are involved lead them into conflict or help them overcome conflict.

Theme

Every successful drama or story reflects a universal theme or emotion. It is this theme or emotion that makes the drama truly meaningful and memorable to the audience. The theme might be something like Justice or Envy or Perseverance or Inevitability.

Emotion

Invoking an emotional response is the foundation of entertainment. Note that being "entertained" does not just mean having "fun." People can be entertained when any of their emotions are engaged. A drama based on a negative emotion such as sadness, anger, jealousy or failure can be every bit as entertaining as one that focuses on laughter, happiness or love. A good drama always reflects a predominant feeling or emotion that the audience can detect (even if unconsciously) as the drama progresses. In an Entertainment–Education drama, the predominant emotion in the main plot should be the one the design team identified in point 6 of the Design Document: the main emotional focus. If the Design Team has determined that a feeling of "hope" will be the most powerful emotion to encourage the audience to make the desired behavior change, then "hope" is the emotion that should be reflected in the main story.

Scene Structure

Not only should the overall story have this dramatic structure, but each scene within an episode also needs a similar structure. Scene structure is especially important in a drama serial where the audience is following several different storylines (or plots) in the various scenes of one episode. Each scene needs to end in suspense, question or doubt, or some feeling that inspires the viewer to want to pick up on that storyline later in the same episode or the following week.

THE 10 PRINCIPLES OF ENTERTAINMENT–EDUCATION PLOT DEVELOPMENT

The following 10 principles provide helpful guidelines for successful Entertainment–Education plot development*:

1. Create an **emotional** experience
2. Tell a **people** story, not a message story
3. Set the story in the local **culture**
4. Stress **concepts** rather than **words**
5. **Demonstrate** rather than lecture

---

*Principles 1–7 are from "Strategies for Improving a Treatment" in *Script Writing for High Impact Videos* by John Morley (published by Wadsworth, 1992). The final three are added as tenets specifically suited to Entertainment–Education writers.

6. Include some **humor**
7. Inspire **positive** change
8. Create **trust** in the recommended change
9. Encourage **advocacy** in the viewing public
10. Create an **original** story

ENHANCING ENTERTAINMENT–EDUCATION DRAMA FOR TELEVISION

One of the major differences between television and film is the place in which each is viewed. A film is generally viewed in a cinema. Because audience members pay to attend the film they are unlikely to walk out before viewing at least a good part of the film. Because the cinema in which the audience sits is almost always dark, everyone's attention is drawn naturally towards the screen—the one bright spot in the theater.

Cinema is, moreover, a social event involving a wide community of people sharing the same experience. These factors (paying to attend, having a main area of focus, and the social experience) are usually not present when the audience watches television in their own homes, either alone or with family and friends. Thus the tendency to be distracted from paying attention to the screen is greater with television than it is with film.

With TV, a quick flick of the switch changes the channel if the viewers are not immediately captured by what they see. The television scriptwriter must keep this in mind. There are certain devices, useful to all drama writers, but of particular importance to the television social drama writer who needs to keep the attention of the audience from the beginning to the end of the story.

Dramatic Devices

The following devices can be helpful in the creation of a powerful drama:

Hook

Some action or unusual happening or event that grabs the audience's attention at the very beginning of the drama or episode. Even if the drama begins on a wide panoramic scene, there must be something in that scene—either immediately or within seconds of the drama beginning—that grabs the audience's attention. This can be an event of nature, such as a tree falling, or it can involve human activity, such as someone running across the screen, or coming out of a doorway onto the street.

Dramatic conflict

The conflict in a drama (or in a narrative story) does not have to be deadly (like a war) or frightening (like an erupting volcano). Dramatic conflict is any situation in which there are two distinctly different sides or points of view, either one of which could predominate or win.

Dramatic conflict typically comes as one of three types:

1. A person against fate; for example, a person trying to survive an earthquake
2. A person (or group of people) against another person (or group of people); for example a householder against a thief, or against a gang of thieves, or a group of students against a political leader or a political party
3. A person against himself or herself; for example, a woman who must decide whether to stay home and look after her family on her husband's low income, or to give the children more in life by taking a job herself.

Jeopardy

In drama this is a combination of dramatic conflict and suspense. The word "jeopardy" means "danger" or "peril." In the original French "jeu parti" means a "divided game" or a situation in which each side in a game had an equal chance of winning or losing. In television drama, "jeopardy" means a situation in which the viewers cannot tell which side will win or which way the story will resolve itself.

Viewers should have a strong feeling that they want the plot to go in one direction, or in favor of one character, but for most of the plot's duration, the resolution is at risk. It is this sense of jeopardy or unresolved conflict that holds the audience's attention.

Suspense

Jeopardy leads to suspense. As the conflict in the story continues to increase, the viewers become more and more anxious for "their side to win," for the conflict to be resolved the way they would like it to end. Even if the viewers are fairly confident that they know how the story will end, there should always be that element of doubt until the last few moments of the climax.

Twists and turns

As a way of encouraging the feeling of jeopardy, it is helpful to introduce unexpected twists and turns into the story.

For example, in the story of the singer (described in Box 4.3), it seemed at first that the teacher wanted the young wife to avoid pregnancy only so that she could win the singing competition and he could earn money and fame by teaching her. The unexpected twist in the story came when he revealed the truth about his own wife. Similarly in the episode from the 156-episode Indian TV drama serial, *Hum Log* (We People) at the end of this chapter, there is an unexpected ironic twist that really captures the audience's attention.

Cliffhanger*

This is a moment of suspense at the end of an act within a drama, or at the end of an episode in a serial drama. Usually a one-hour television drama episode is broken into four scenes, so that between one scene and the next there is room for a commercial. In a one-hour stand-alone television drama, the cliffhanger should come in the middle of the hour, between scenes 2 and 3. If the program is only half an hour long, the drama will be divided into two scenes and the cliffhanger will come at the end of the first scene. In the case of a half-hour serial drama where the story continues from week to week, there should be a minor cliffhanger, or at least an unanswered "question" at the end of each scene and a major cliffhanger at the end of each episode.

Recurrent behaviors

One way to help ensure that the message does not dominate over the story is through the recurrent behaviors of some of the characters. Recurrent behaviors are like irrelevant, but interesting, bits of trimming on a garment. They run throughout the story and serve the main purpose of ensuring that the characters behave like real people; people the audience could know in real life. They also allow the audience the joy of anticipation.

For example, in the Bangladeshi Entertainment–Education serial drama, *Shyamol Chaya,* the character of the village leader, Kuddus, has the strange habit of hiccuping every time he tells a lie.

This habit is of no great importance to the plot, but it turns Kuddus into a real and somewhat humorous character. The audience anticipates this quirk each time Kuddus comes on the screen, feeling that they know the character well enough to predict what he will do. For some characters a recurrent behavior can be a verbal expression that they use frequently, such as a servant saying "Forgive me, forgive me, forgive me" every time he interrupts his master.

Recurrent behaviors can also relate to locations and scenery: a car door that is extremely difficult to open; a tap that sprays water in the face of whoever turns it on, etc.

Before considering the use of dramatic devices, however, the writer begins with a strong story idea.

---

*The word "cliffhanger" originated with movie serials that were shown on Saturday afternoons in the early days of American cinema. These serials often involved cowboy heroes trying to escape their enemies (very often American Indians). Frequently, the episode would end with a cowboy leaping over a cliff in an attempt to escape. The movie would close with the cowboy hanging on to the edge of the cliff. The audience was left in suspense till the next week, waiting to know if the cowboy would be rescued or would fall to his death from his cliffhanging position.

Starting the Story

Writers who are commissioned to script an Entertainment–Education drama begin with acceptance of the fact that their primary purpose is not to establish themselves as great writers, but to create drama that will give ordinary people the chance to improve their lives. Next, writers have a clear understanding of the audience to whom the behavior change message is directed, and an appreciation of the type of drama that audience enjoys: action, mystery, love story, tragedy, etc. It is difficult to use a story that is entirely comedy for Entertainment–Education purposes, because an important message delivered in a comic way might be less likely to be taken seriously by the audience. It is possible, even essential, to include some humor (perhaps in the form of one humorous character) in almost every Entertainment–Education drama serial. A well-drawn humorous character appeals to virtually every audience, and a good writer will find a way to add a little humor to the most serious of stories. (Consider the character of the Fool in Shakespeare's tragedy, *King Lear*).

Suiting the Story to the Audience

Writers should spend time with their intended audiences and observe their daily living environment and habits, understand their concerns, and learn to appreciate what is of value to them. At the design workshop, writers learn a great deal about the audience and their relationship to the problem to be addressed in the drama. Only by spending time with the people for whom they are writing, however, can they truly understand the personal and daily lives of their audiences.

Some writers like to include on the writing team someone from the audience for whom they are writing, such as a young writer for programs designed for an adolescent audience. There is some wisdom in that approach, but it is not essential: Shakespeare was not an adolescent when he wrote one of the world's most famous adolescent stories: *Romeo and Juliet*. The primary essential attribute an Entertainment–Education writer must possess is the ability to write really good drama. It is important, of course, to check as the writing goes ahead that the type of story being written appeals to the intended audience.

Gender-specific appeal

It seems that in almost every country in the world there is a difference in the type of stories enjoyed by women and by men. As a wide generalisation, men tend to prefer action and some degree of macho display (an exaggerated sense of strong, physical masculinity), while women tend more towards love stories and stories of human tragedy. Both men and women seem to enjoy mystery. The Entertainment–Education writer must be sure to have an understanding of the type of story that will appeal most to the audience for whom the messages are intended.

Similarly, in some cultures, it is the fathers or husbands who are the "gatekeepers"—the ones who decide what programs will be viewed or listened to each day. In many countries, parents determine the programs their children—even adolescent children—can watch. If this is true of the project's chosen audiences, writers should ensure that their stories have initial appeal to these gatekeepers. The *Jasoos Vijay* serial was deliberately designed with a detective as the main character, because the program planners knew this would appeal to the male audience they wanted to reach.

Similarly, the Indonesian writer, Jujur Pranato, was commissioned to write a 3-part television drama that could blend in important and powerful messages on safe motherhood. Jujur knew he had to appeal strongly to a male audience in order to encourage men to watch the series and thereby allow their wives to watch as both of them learned how to take the best possible care of pregnant women. He knew, also, that he must write a story that would contain dramatic visual events that would work well on television.

He chose, therefore, to write a mystery, *Flowers for Nur,* knowing that he could bring into the plot a lot of action that would appeal to his male viewers. He set the opening scene of the mystery in a village mobile cinema. One of the film viewers at the mobile cinema, a young man named Adek, goes away from the crowd for a few moments to smoke a cigarette. Outside the cinema, he gets into a brief physical fight with another man, Usep. The audience is not made aware of the cause of this fight, which is over quite quickly. Adek does not return to the cinema and after the show his dead body is found in a nearby river. The audience is immediately suspicious that he has been murdered by Usep. This opening action hooks the viewers—especially the men—who want to know what the fight was about and how and why the murder (if it was that) took place.

Suiting the Story to the Medium and the Message

The next step for Jujur in *Flowers for Nur* was to blend the message into his plot naturally and gradually and subtly. This he did through the character of Nur, the wife of Usep, the chief murder suspect. Nur is pregnant and someone in the village is spreading rumors that the father of the child is not Usep, but the dead man, Adek. As various people in the village are questioned by the police, the audience learns that Adek had indeed wanted to marry Nur. He had gone away to the city to earn a good living with which to start his married life. While he was away working for a clinic in the city, Nur's family insisted that it was time for her to marry and they arranged a union with Usep.

When Adek returned to the village, he saw that Usep and his mother were not caring for Nur properly. He began to take care of her himself, escorting her for her antenatal visits and insisting that she should have good food and not work too hard. Several of the villagers, as well as the village head and the local midwife all report to the police on the type of care that Adek is demanding for Nur, and this helps to stress, quite naturally, the type of care that every pregnant woman should be given. This part of the story accomplished two things at once: it allowed the message to come in naturally and to be repeated several times, and it intensified the suspense in the plot. The audience, like many people in the village, began to wonder about Adek's motives in taking such care of Nur, and began to suspect that Usep must have killed him, believing him to be the father of Nur's child. At the same time, the policeman in charge of the investigation made a point of ensuring that everyone treated the pregnant Nur with special care whenever she was brought in for questioning.

The story has a happy ending. Usep confesses his suspicions to Nur as she goes into labor. She is able to persuade him that his suspicions are groundless. Nur goes through a successful delivery because of all the care she has had. The baby is born healthy. It is learned subsequently that Adek was not murdered, but that he slipped into the river when he went to pick some flowers for Nur. He was killed when he hit his head on a rock as he slipped down the river bank.

One of the most interesting features of this trilogy was that the whole story was seen through the eyes of a young girl, Entin, who both contributed to and helped solve the mystery. She also provided some humorous moments in the story, and she added the "character quirk" to the story, as she worked on her favourite hobby: modelling with clay. While making a clay model of her own village and the activities she saw in it, she inadvertently revealed certain clues that helped to solve the mystery. At the same time, the audience had the opportunity to pick up on these clues and they began to solve the mystery themselves.

Plot Clues

In any story—not just in a mystery—the audience needs to have a chance to figure out how the plot will unfold. There should be clues, even very subtle clues, in the plot line, so that when the resolution finally unfolds, the audience can realize that indeed—given the plot clues—the story *had to* unfold this way.

Avoid "Deus Ex Machina"

This Greek term means "god from a machine." In early Greek drama, at the moment of crisis, a machine literally delivered the god character onto the stage to resolve the problem. In modern drama, *deus ex machina* means a character or contrived event that suddenly appears or happens to resolve the conflict. While this might have been exciting in early Greek stage drama, in modern drama it is usually very disappointing to an audience. They like (and need) to be able to become involved in the plot and work out the ending for themselves. For example: Having a leading character suddenly die from a deadly disease about which the audience knew nothing and had no prior clues leaves the audience feeling cheated. Even if the audience dislike the way a drama ends, they should be able to think back over it and conclude "Yes, I can see why it had to end this way."

Detailed Episode Synopsis for Television Serial Drama

Once the general outline of a television serial drama has been approved by the review team, the writer begins work on the detailed outline of each episode, scene by scene, showing clearly where the message will come in.

The Story Synopsis

No writer should ever undertake the writing of the script of an Entertainment–Education film or the episodes of a drama serial without first creating the synopsis. Without the carefully crafted synopsis, it is all too easy to leave out important parts of the message, or to run into serious difficulties of inserting the message naturally in the sequence required by the design document. The synopsis is particularly important for a serial drama because the serial contains several plots and continues over a period of time. Unless the synopsis is worked through in detail, it is easy to confuse the roles of the various characters or even omit some accidentally. It is also easy for the time lines of the various plots to become confused if the writer tries to work on the episodes without first completing a detailed synopsis. This can result in having one plot in which the action could be completed in six months and a separate plot that requires at least a year of story time to reach its conclusion.

The synopsis (which does not contain dialogue) should show clearly the various plots of the drama, the main message, or topic, that each plot will carry, the predominant emotion of each plot and the details of the main characters in each plot. Television and film synopses, therefore, are based on the following plot development guidelines:

Plot Development

For each plot in the drama, the synopsis should clearly reveal:

- **The characters** and their personalities
- **The main conflict** and how it is resolved
- **The main message(s)** that each plot will deliver
- **The location** of the plot
- **The time** that is covered from beginning to end of the plot, making sure that all plots fit into the same timeline
- plots fit into the same timeline
- **The main emotion** each plot will reflect

The following sample (of the first two episodes of a 26-part drama) is taken from the Vietnam television serial, *Overcoming Challenge*. Note that in the first episode, there is no specific health message; the writers use the first episode to establish the story. In episode 2, the writers have clearly identified where the message will come in Scene 3.

Note also that the writers have marked one scene in each episode as an **optional cut**. In the event that the episode is too long after filming, this is the scene that can be cut during editing. It is helpful for these optional cuts to be selected by the writer, who can ensure that removing the chosen scene will have no adverse effect on the message.

OVERCOMING CHALLENGE

EPISODE 1

Scene 1:　**Typical scene: Hanoi, West Lake. (Main plot introduction)**

Quang and his girlfriend Ngan are walking together on their way to the house of Mr Thep (Quang's father). We see that they are lovers by the way they are looking at each other, holding hands, etc. In their conversation, the audience learns that there is a disagreement between them about an aspect of their forthcoming wedding (this will come up again in the final episode). In this scene we also learn that Ngan works with a newspaper, and Quang works for a youth agency, but we do not learn exactly what Quang does. As they approach the house, the audience is made aware that Quang does not want Ngan to discuss his work with his family.

Scene 2:　**At the gate of Mr Thep's house, daytime.**

A car has just stopped in front of the gate. Mr Thep and his employee Mr Loc, along with the driver, Tien (the main character in subplot A), get out of the car and walk into the house. Mr Thep's younger daughter, Dien (12 years old) happily welcomes her father as a girl who has been spoiled by the parents. Mr Loc says hello to Dien and praises her that she has grown up so quickly. Dien doesn't want to be praised like a kid as she thinks she has grown up already. Dien asks Tien to teach her how to drive the car. Tien promises to teach her but he cannot do it now because he has to go on a business mission.

Scene 3:　**In the dining room of Mr Thep's house, daytime.**

At a lunch on Saturday, there are Mr and Mrs Thep, Dien, Mrs Chi (Mrs Thep's sister, and a main character in subplot B) and her daughter Mai, and Mr Loc. Mr Thep introduces Mrs Chi (who lives in a rural area and visits her sister on weekends) to Mr Loc. Everyone is treated with simple dishes brought by Mrs Chi from her rural home. When everyone is having lunch, Quang and Ngan arrive and sit down to lunch. Mr Thep asks Quang about his job; he quickly changes the subject and asks Mai (who lives with the Theps) how she is getting on with her preparations for the singing competition.

Scene 4:   In the bedroom of Mai and Dien after lunch, daytime. (subplot C)

Mai is lying on the bed and reading an article, which praises the artist, Dinh. Dien is trying on a skirt and looks at herself in the mirror. She makes a wry face and thinks that she doesn't look like other fashionable girls. Dien asks Mai for her comments but Mai answers very carelessly because she is busy reading the article. Dien is angry and she seizes the newspaper. Seeing Dinh's photo, Dien begins to tease Mai, who seems to be attracted to Dinh.

Scene 5:   In the bedroom of Quang, daytime.

Quang, Ngan, Dinh are sitting and talking about the football match which is to happen the next afternoon. Quang says he supports the Shield Club and hopes that the Club will be the champion one round earlier if it wins over the Lightning Club tomorrow. Dinh doesn't like football and teases that only stupid people would pay attention to the ball in the yard. The two provoke each other. Ngan finds it funny to follow the humorous argument between the two men. Mr Thep calls them to come to the living room to have tea.

The men continue to discuss football. Mr Thep supports the Lightning Club. So he, Thep, and Quang bet for the winner of next day's match. Mrs Thep says it would be better for the men to bet about who will give up smoking first. She says this is her major concern. Mr Thep and Quang are forced to put out their cigarettes. Mr Thep asks Quang if he is doing a story on betting. He says yes, but it is obvious to the audience that he is hiding something.

Scene 6:   At the discotheque, evening.

Quang and Ngan are dancing at a discotheque. Ngan follows two girls to the toilet. A few minutes later she returns to Quang and tells him that those girls asked her if she wanted to buy the drug, ecstasy. When the two girls leave the discotheque, Quang signals Ngan saying that they should follow the girls. He tells Ngan that this is what he is researching for his assignment where he works at the Youth Research Center—drug use by young people. She says she will write an article on the topic for her newspaper.

Scene 7:   In the street, evening (*football café*).

The two girls enter a football café. Many young men are gathering inside the café. Quang and Ngan stop and look inside the place and then continue walking. Ngan wants to enter the place but Quang says it is not good. Ngan is angry and thinks that Quang cannot do things properly. Quang tries to reconcile with her.

Scene 8: **In the living room of Mr Thep's house, evening.**

Discussion between the sisters: Mrs Chi is talking about her son-in-law, Huy (married to her elder daughter, Phuong) who, with financial support from his relatives, has been studying mechanical engineering in Ho Chi Minh City. He is now about to return home permanently. Phuong is 6 months pregnant because they knew that with Huy's new skills, they could afford to have a second child.

OPTIONAL CUT SCENE

Scene 9: **Mr Thep's house. The bedroom of Dien and Mai, daytime.**

Mrs Chi is telling Mai of the work that girls should do around the house. Mai doesn't like it because her mother talks too much. Mai thinks there are many differences between her generation and her mother's, especially when Mrs Chi always thinks like a rural woman. Mrs Chi is very sad to hear her daughter say this.

Scene 10: **Football café (which was discovered by Quang and Ngan last night), daytime.**

Quang and Dinh enter under the watchful eyes of the young boys in the café because it is their first visit to the place. Quang intentionally shows off, as if he is very fashionable, to distract others' attention. He calls for a beer and cigarettes. On the screen is the football match between the Lightning and the Shield. According to Quang and Dinh, it seems that the match goes on unusually long. Quang sees two boys going out to the toilet. He follows them and sees they are sniffing drugs. He stands quietly by the door, watching. Somebody (unseen to the audience) taps him on the shoulder. He reacts in a startled, almost frightened manner.

END OF EPISODE 1

EPISODE 2

Scene 1: **At a bar, evening.**

Pick up from last episode. The person who tapped Quang on the shoulder is only trying to get to the toilet to get drugs. Quang returns to his seat and then, when they leave, he follows the drug people.

Scene 2: **In the secret lane.**

He sees many young people there buying drugs. Sees a young boy, Vu, there.

Scene 3: **At a refreshment shop on the pavement, morning.**

Quang and Ngan are having breakfast. They talk about the young boys using drugs. They discuss the reasons that make them become drug addicts

(*Message: Reasons leading to drug addiction.*) Ngan says Quang is taking risks with this assignment. Quang becomes very passionate on the topic of why young people take drugs. He can't understand why they would risk killing themselves. Ngan tries to calm him down, but he remains passionate. She promises to try help his cause with the article she is writing.

Scene 4:   **At Mr Thep's house, at night.**
Mr and Mrs Thep and Mrs Chi are talking about Mai's prospects at the coming singing contest. Mr Thep takes out a cigarette and Mrs Thep reminds him of his promise to quit smoking. Mr Thep has to put away his cigarettes. (**Anti-smoking and anti-alcohol messages will run throughout the drama.**)

Scene 5:   **At Hung Thinh Company, daytime.**
Mr Thep is telling Tien to prepare the car for a long trip. Tien is humorous when talking about his career and his dislike of women. Tien leaves.

Scene 6:   **At the headquarters of *Thanh Xuan* newspaper (where Ngan works), daytime.**
Ngan is talking to Phu—the line manager and senior reporter (and woman chaser) at the newspaper where she works. Ngan tells Phu about her intended article on drugs. He half agrees; half disagrees. Phu warns her to be cautious. This scene reveals a lot about their characters and their relationship. Phu is flirting with her. She is polite but does not encourage him.

Scene 7:   **At the Youth Research Institute, daytime.**
At Quang's working room, he is talking to everybody about the scene he saw in the secret lane. Quang says he will investigate the gang to support his study. Du (who works in the same room with Quang and is a few years older), asks in detail about the case. Quang innocently reveals the location of the lane. Du is stunned for a second but nobody notices. All people discuss drug abuse and the causes that push people to drug addiction (*continue the message: information about where to go for drug help comes in here.*)

Scene 8:   **University, daytime.**
Mai performs a song in front of her teachers before attending the contest. Dinh is among the persons who are watching her and he seems to be pleased with the song presented by Mai. Dinh and Mai discuss the singing contest and he encourages her. It is clear that Mai is infatuated by him.

OPTIONAL CUT SCENE

Scene 9:   **Thep's house, daytime.**

Tien is helping Mrs Thep and Mrs Chi to bring home the things they bought at a supermarket. Tien is working while asking about Quang and tries to praise Quang. Mrs Thep is somewhat embarrassed by his praise. Mrs Chi asks about Tien's wife and children. But Tien is humorously talking about how he avoids women and he makes the two women laugh.

Scene 10:   **At the Youth Research Institute, daytime.**

Deputy Director of the Institute, Mr Tan, summons Quang and informs him that he is going to give the study **"On the situation of drug addiction among young people"** to another person. He stresses that this is a complicated study and that it is the focal point of the Institute for this year. He says that Quang is too young to have enough experience to handle it, therefore he is afraid that Quang may not succeed. Quang is angry, asks a number of questions and then leaves abruptly.

END OF EPISODE 2

The same detailed outline was completed for ALL episodes of the drama before actual script writing commenced.

5

ARTISTRY
Character Development

Photograph by Harvey Nelson

Good writers bring their characters to life in several ways.

THE IMPORTANCE OF CHARACTERS

While a strong plot is essential to a successful drama, of equal importance are the characters who implement the plot. The choice of characters is highly significant in Entertainment–Education drama because the characters must be not only relevant to the plot, they must also be truly appropriate to the audience, and at least some of them must operate as role-models for the audience. This is not to say that all characters must be exact replicas of people from the chosen audience, but their lifestyles, their clothing, their general demeanor must be recognizable and acceptable to the audience.

All fictional characters are exaggerations of real life, largely because all aspects of their lives have to be revealed in such a limited time span. In a weekly television drama with 20- or 30-minute episodes, the leading characters are probably seen by their audience for a maximum of 12–15 minutes a week, and more often, the leading characters are on the screen for less than half the broadcast time of each episode. The time span covered by the story in a 26-episode serial is usually not more than a few months. How can the writer make a character who has so little "contact" with the audience into a realistic and unforgettable person? The secret lies in writers knowing their characters so well that they cannot help revealing a full and detailed picture even within a limited episode length.

The 6 Points of Personal Life of Characters

Many successful writers base their characters on people they know personally or on people they meet in visits to the chosen audience's environment. In order to be sure of developing a character completely and realistically, an Entertainment–Education writer should develop and write down a detailed profile for each major character. Although many of these details might never be mentioned in the drama, the writer needs to be aware of them in order to make the characters real (see Box 5.1). The following points should be covered:

1. Past life

Even if a character is 40 years old when she appears in the story, the writer should compile a detailed description of her past life, covering such matters as:

- where she was born
- how many brothers and sisters she has and where she is in the family line up: youngest, oldest, middle, etc.
- how much education she had and how well she did at school
- any traumatic events in her past life (such as the death of her mother at an early age)
- any major illnesses she has had
- her age at marriage
- what jobs she has held (if any)
- how many pregnancies and live births she has had
- what her dreams were as a child and to what extent these dreams have or have not come true

2. Present life

This can be divided into two categories in some cases (depending on the character and the culture)

Personal

The writer should compile as many details as possible of the character's life at home:

- Married or single; state of the marriage if married
- Number and sex of children
- Hobbies
- Religion
- Social activities
- Things that give pleasure and things that cause concern or unhappiness
- Dreams for the future
- Closest friends
- State of health
- Personal habits (such as always being late for appointments or being forgetful about small details, or liking certain foods)
- Present appearance: weight; height; features

Professional life

- Job
- Hours worked each day and days each week
- Place of work
- Attitude to job
- How many years in this job
- Salary: low, high, medium (sufficient or insufficient for a good living)
- Ambition and prospects on the job
- What the character likes and dislikes most about the job
- Attitude of boss to the character, or attitude of the character (as the boss) to other people

Box 5.1

THE 6 POINTS OF PERSON PRESENTATION

1. Past life
2. Present life
3. Professional life
4. Private life
5. Personality characteristic
6. Passion

4. Private life

This reveals the side of the character that is not seen by family, friends or co-workers. For example:

- What does the character do when alone: read books; try out different hairstyles; sleep at the slightest opportunity; spy on other members of the family or on neighbors; pray; write letters; play with pet animals (dog, cat) etc.?
- What does the character say or think when alone? A character can reveal a lot through innermost thoughts that are not revealed to other characters. These thoughts can be revealed to the audience through such actions as: writing in a diary; talking to a pet; writing letters to a distant friend; talking to a baby.

5. Personality quirk or characteristic

What is the main personality quirk or characteristic that is the strongest motivator of what the person does? It is often this personality characteristic that drives the plot of the story. A character's behavior might be driven by jealousy of another character or by egotism or by an overwhelming desire to help other people. For example, in the story of *Flowers for Nur* (pages 92–93), it was the jealous nature of Usep, the cruel nature of the mother, and the overprotective nature of Adek that led the characters into conflict and that motivated the actions of the plot. It was the streak of curiosity in Entin's personality that helped to solve the mystery.

6. Passion

The leading characters in well-structured drama always have a particular "passion" in life. It is usually this "passion" that leads to the dilemma or jeopardy in the story and brings about the real crisis in the life of the character.

The most successful story writers are those who know their characters like close personal friends and who can reveal the true natures of the characters through what the characters say and do, how they react to situations, and how other people react to and treat them. Telling the story of their characters is as compelling for good writers as talking about their own lives. In order to tell their characters' stories in a convincing manner, writers must spend considerable time becoming thoroughly acquainted with these 6 points of the characters' lives.

Making "Message Characters" Real

An all too frequent mistake that writers make in social development dramas is presenting "message characters" (such as nurses, doctors, and those who carry or role model the main messages) as perfect or unreal people. Audiences will have much greater trust in these characters if they are truly human and believable. At the end of this chapter is an episode from the Indian Entertainment–Education drama "Hum Log." This episode is an excellent demonstration of two very important features of good social change drama: (1) A truly human and believable "message character"; and (2) an excellent use of irony.* Not only does the audience trust and believe in the Lady Doctor as a real person, they inevitably develop genuine sympathy and concern for what seems like gross unfairness in her life. They will want to watch future episodes as much to find out what happens to the message-carrying Lady Doctor as to see what happens to other characters in the story.

Attracting the Audience to the Characters and the Message

This *Hum Log* episode admirably demonstrates the following important points of good Entertainment–Education writing:

- natural and realistic inclusion of the message
- gentle humor (grandmother in scene 1)
- a realistic and believable "message character"—The Lady Doctor
- male involvement in women's lives
- an ending that has both emotion and an unanswered question: what will the future hold for the Lady Doctor?

---

*Irony is the state of incongruity, or discordance between what the audience expects and what actually happens.

Character Demonstration: Hum Log

HUM LOG. Episode # 5   *(Originally written in Hindi)*

ACT ONE

INT. FAMILY'S INFORMAL LIVING ROOM—EVENING

(CHUTKI IS READING A BOOK. SHE HEARS A VOICE; RAISES HER HEAD)

1. GRANDMOTHER   Hey, Chutki, do you want to spoil your eyes by reading in the dark.

    (GRANDMOTHER TURNS ON THE LAMP, AND BOWS TO THE LAMP IN REVERENCE)

    Stop reading. This is the time for cows to return home. This time is only for the purpose of worshipping God. Do not do anything else.

2. CHUTKI   I am at this time worshipping the goddess of knowledge.

    (GRANDMOTHER SITS BY CHUTKI'S SIDE, AND FIDDLES WITH HER BOOKS)

3. GRANDMOTHER   What will this education result in? At the time of marriage, prospective parties only see whether the girl is proficient in cooking and cleaning. Badki was educated till class 12 and that's the reason she hasn't been married. The other day, heaven knows what she said in *English* to her prospective groom, that he rejected her.

4. CHUTKI   The groom rejected Badki not because she spoke in English, but because of the dowry. Badki spoke English only on his insistence. These days, grandmother, grooms prefer convent educated and working women. Poor Badki passed her high school in the first division. If she studies further, and gets a job, she will get married without any problems.

5. GRANDMOTHER   You are right about the grooms these days. They want their wives to accompany them to hotels for dancing, and jump into the pond wearing silmilling suits.

6. CHUTKI	(SMILING) Not silmilling! swimming suits, grandmother.
7. GRANDMOTHER	(WAVING HER HANDS) Don't try to teach me English. I have seen women wearing silmilling suits even before your father was born. I am the wife of an armyman. My life has been spent in cantonments. After living with you I have started forgetting my English. Otherwise my English was so good that I used to fluently converse with memsahibs (*English women*).
8. CHUTKI	(AMUSED) Of course.
9. GRANDMOTHER	The commander's wife would say to me in English, "Hey you Hawaldar's wife." And I would reply, "Yes Sir."
10. CHUTKI	(LAUGHING) Women are not called Sir, they are called Madam.
11. GRANDMOTHER	If they were any Jill or Jane, you can call them anything. These Englishwomen were such amazons that nobody could dare call them Madam.
12. CHUTKI	I did not know, grandmother, that you know English. Keep it up.
13. GRANDMOTHER	What up keep? What should I pick up and keep.

(CHUTKI LAUGHS AT HER GRANDMOTHER'S BROKEN ENGLISH)

	Don't laugh. I know a lot of English by rote.
14. CHUTKI	Grandmother, grandmother, please let me read.

(GRANDMOTHER PATS CHUTKI'S CHEEKS SOFTLY)

15. GRANDMOTHER	If you read a lot, you would start to wear glasses. Once you have glasses nobody would marry you.

(CHUTKI GETS UP TO LEAVE)

16. CHUTKI	So let them not marry me. I don't want to marry; I want to be a medical doctor. Bye-bye, English grandmother. I will now go and study inside.

(GRANDMOTHER HOLDS CHUTKI AND MAKES HER SIT)

17 GRANDMOTHER Sit and talk to me, little one. In this house, I can never find anybody to sit and talk with me. Your mother locks her mouth, and spends most of her time in the kitchen. Your grandfather spends most of his time with his good-for-nothing friends. They all read newspapers, and curse the entire world. Why don't people take more interest in their homes? Your father drowns his sorrows in booze. You kids never stay at home. In the daytime, you all come home and fight, and go away. In the night, you all sleep like horses. We all should sit together and share our joys and sorrows.

18 CHUTKI Grandmother, this house is so small that when everybody is here it is like a traffic jam. Where is the place for everybody to sit and talk?

19 GRANDMOTHER There should be place in one's heart. When I got married there were 45 people in my grandfather's house. There were so many people that I couldn't even talk to your grandfather properly. I had to keep my eyes down all the time. I found a way to talk to him by moving my toes.

(GRANDMOTHER WIGGLES HER TOES)

20. CHUTKI (POINTS TO HER GRANDMOTHER'S TOES)
What does wiggling of the toes mean?

21. GRANDMOTHER The one who had to understand, understood.

(SOUND OF A CAR HORN. CHUTKI RISES)

22. CHUTKI It seems Jeejaji (brother-in-law) has arrived. Now I will not be able to study.

(BROTHER-IN-LAW, RAM ANJOR, AND PREGNANT SISTER RAJJO COME IN AND EXCHANGE GREETINGS. RAJJO TOUCHES THE FEET OF THE GRANDMOTHER. GRANDMOTHER HUGS RAM ANJOR)

23. RAM ANJOR Greetings, grandmother.

24. GRANDMOTHER Have a long life, son. I feel very happy when I meet you.

(RAJJO MOVES TOWARDS THE KITCHEN)

| 25. RAJJO | Mother, you must be in the kitchen. Mother...are you there? |

(RAM ANJOR HUGS CHUTKI)

26. CHUTKI	So Jeejaji, you've driven here in a borrowed car?
27. RAM ANJOR	We mechanics sit in others' cars with our own wives. The people who own these cars sit with others' wives. So, did you give my message to the "High Command?" Are my in-laws making arrangements for the money?
28. GRANDMOTHER	Son, these days Rajjo's father is not doing well financially. But he will still do something.
29. RAM ANJOR	If there is money left after his drinking, then only will he do something, no?
	(TALKS TO CHUTKI) You left two days ago but didn't come back. We kept remembering you, "heroine."
30. CHUTKI	I am not the "heroine"; the "heroine" is Majhli.
31. RAM ANJOR	Which sister-in-law is not a "heroine" for a Jeeja? If the Jeeja is a hero.
32. CHUTKI	But Jeeja is a zero.
33. RAM ANJOR	Jeeja is a hero. Do you know the full details of my romance with your sister, Rajjo?

(RAJJO'S VOICE IN THE BACKGROUND).

34. RAJJO	What romance? Whose romance?
35. RAM ANJOR	Ours.
36. RAJJO	Do we have a love story?!!!!!!
37. RAM ANJOR	Why not? And each of your sisters knows our love story. Chutki, let's hear the first scene of the latest Romeo-Juliet in town.
38. CHUTKI	Our brother-in-law...
39. RAM ANJOR	I wasn't your brother-in-law then.
40. CHUTKI	Our would-be brother-in-law, Mr RAM ANJOR, a motor mechanic, was lying under a car.

41.	RAM ANJOR	Imported car.
42.	CHUTKI	Please don't interrupt so much. So Rajjo and Badki were passing by the side of Jeeja's car. They did not see native legs sticking out from under an imported car. So Rajjo tripped and fell.
43.	GRANDMOTHER	Son, Ram Anjor, your wife is expecting. It is dangerous for her to fall.
44.	RAJJO	This happened before we got married, grandmother.
45.	GRANDMOTHER	It might have happened before, but what kind of a man is he? How could he stick his leg out, and make a woman trip on it?
46.	RAJJO	Grandmother, he didn't do it on purpose, I didn't see his legs.
47.	GRANDMOTHER	Tomorrow you will say you can't see a car. You should watch and walk.
48.	RAM ANJOR	If she watched and walked, how could she have met me?
49.	RAJJO	(JOKING) I wouldn't have had the misfortune of marrying you.
50.	GRANDMOTHER	Tripping and falling is no joking matter.
51.	CHUTKI	This is a love story, grandmother.
52.	GRANDMOTHER	What story?
53.	RAM ANJOR	You will have difficulty understanding this. This is youthful talk.
54.	GRANDMOTHER	Dear child, who told you that I straight away became an old woman, and that I was never youthful? By God's grace, and thanks to clarified butter, your grandmother is, even now, more youthful than people like you. Now tell me what "youthful" talk you were referring to?
55.	RAM ANJOR	This is a love story, grandma, love story.
56.	GRANDMOTHER	Lup story, now I understand. Lup, my son, is romance in English. And romance is not a laughing matter, it is a crying matter.
57.	RAM ANJOR	(LAUGHING) All right!!!!

58. GRANDMOTHER   Of course, Rajjo's grandfather showed me many silent movies on love.

59. CHUTKI   Did you have to wiggle your toes to tell grandpa that you wanted to see movies?

60. GRANDMOTHER   Shut up, Chutki. You are pint-sized, and you are worried about my wiggling toes. Lup-jhup, wiggling toes, romance, it is a heart's maze. There was one romantic play that Rajjo's father saw five times. Durgadas was the lead player.

61. RAM ANJOR   No, Grandma, it was Devdas.

62. GRANDMOTHER   Devdas or Durgadas, he died in the play an unhappy person. There were two women who had endeared themselves to this man; both cried endlessly. So did the audience.

(EVERYBODY LAUGHS)

This is not a laughing matter.

63. RAJJO   I know, Grandma, I know....

(RAJJO HOLDS HER BELLY, AND SCREAMS IN PAIN)

64. CHUTKI   What happened, Rajjo sister?

65. GRANDMOTHER   Nothing happened. Something will happen now. My great-grandson. Son Ram Anjor, take her to the hospital immediately.

(RAM ANJOR TOUCHES GRANDMA'S FEET)

66. RAM ANJOR   I hope your prophecy works out right. RAM ANJOR, the father of many daughters, may he return as the father of a son.

(FADE OUT. COMMERCIAL BREAK)

ACT TWO

INT. HOSPITAL, LADY DOCTOR'S CLINIC—NIGHT

(LADY DOCTOR COMES OUT FROM BEHIND THE SCREEN WIPING HER HANDS. RAJJO IS FOLLOWING HER. RAM ANJOR RISES FROM THE BENCH)

1.	LADY DOCTOR	(SITS ON HER CHAIR) Rajjo doesn't have regular labor pains yet. Take her home. If she has pains again, get her to the hospital.
2.	RAM ANJOR	When will the pain start again?
3.	LADY DOCTOR	(ASKS BOTH TO SIT DOWN) We cannot be sure, but we will do what we can to relieve the pain for her. Labor could start after one day, two days. It will come when it is time. (PAUSE) By the way, how many children do you have already?
4.	RAM ANJOR	Thanks to you, she has three daughters.
5.	LADY DOCTOR	Why thanks to me? I would suggest 3 is enough. Perhaps you should have a vasectomy or your wife should have a tubectomy. You already have three daughters. You will have another one. Four are enough, for anyone to care for.
6.	RAM ANJOR	Please don't say that I will have another daughter. I pray to God that I have a son.
7.	LADY DOCTOR	I will pray to God also. Right now I pray to you to think about the size of your family. Ensure that you or your wife adopt a permanent family planning method before it is too late.
8.	RAM ANJOR	Even the government says one can have 2 or 3, or even 5 children.
9.	LADY DOCTOR	(IMPATIENTLY) You are making 5 out of 3. And this is a very old slogan. Nowadays most people believe that husband-wife and one child is enough to make a perfect family.
10.	RAM ANJOR	Is it essential to have the operation right now? We will get it done later.
11.	LADY DOCTOR	It is not essential that a tubectomy should be performed only at the time of childbirth. It can be done any time. But if the

woman is in a hospital for childbirth, it is both convenient and safe to have the tubectomy performed then. So what do you say, shall we perform the tubectomy?

12.	RAM ANJOR	If it is a boy, we can think about it.
13.	LADY DOCTOR	Not if it is a girl? How many daughters will you produce to try for a son?
14.	RAM ANJOR	It is Rajjo who produces the daughters. From my own side, I always request she produce the carrier of the family name: one who brings honor to the family.
15.	LADY DOCTOR	It is the sperm of the man which decides the sex of the child. The woman's body has no effect on the sex of the child. Besides, don't daughters bring honor to the family? Didn't Sita bring honor to King Janak?
16.	RAM ANJOR	Hail Janak, and hail Sita.
17.	LADY DOCTOR	O.K. then you think about the tubectomy. There are two women sitting in this room, and you chauvinistic men are saying that it is useless to have daughters.
18.	RAM ANJOR	This is my problem. In the house there are four female votes, against my one. To strengthen my party I need just four sons.
19.	RAJJO	Four sons!! No, I can't do it.
20.	RAM ANJOR	At least one.
21.	RAJJO	If it is in our fate, we will have a son this time. No more after this. We can't even feed these four properly.
22.	RAM ANJOR	Will you listen to me, Madam?
23.	RAJJO	No, I will not listen to you. Listening to you I have become like this.
24.	LADY DOCTOR	Please debate this matter at home. I would urge you to get a tubectomy performed. Why your husband can't agree, I fail to understand.
25.	RAM ANJOR	Lady doctor, with God's grace, you must be having lots of sons playing in your garden. How will you understand my predicament?

(LADY DOCTOR DOESN'T REPLY. SHE STARTS COLLECTING HER PAPERS)

26.	RAJJO	Lady doctor, how many sons and daughters do you have?
27.	LADY DOCTOR	None.
28.	RAJJO	Didn't you marry?
29.	LADY DOCTOR	I have been married for 17 years.
30.	RAJJO	Tomorrow my younger sister, Lajjo, will celebrate her fifth wedding anniversary. She doesn't have any children, either. They say they are planning their family. But you couldn't have planned for 17 years?
31.	LADY DOCTOR	I cannot have a child. Please leave me alone. Please go.

(RAM ANJOR AND RAJJO RISE TO GO)

32.	RAM ANJOR	If you so order, I will get you Swami Keharia's magic powder. If you have this powder with betel leaf, it will remove infertility.
33.	LADY DOCTOR	(ANGRY) Worry about your wife, not me. Take her home immediately, and let her rest.

(THEY LEAVE. LADY DOCTOR PUTS HER HEAD IN HER HANDS. TELEPHONE RINGS. SHE PICKS UP THE PHONE)

Hello. Yes this is Doctor Aparna Zahir. No I don't have any time for a medical round tomorrow.

(BANGS THE PHONE DOWN. SHE TRIES TO CALL SOMEONE. NO LUCK)

Damn, this blasted phone!!!

(CALLS ANOTHER NUMBER. IS LUCKY THIS TIME).

Hello Bula, this is Doctor Zahir. If you make coffee, please send me a cup. My head is hurting.

(LADY DOCTOR PUTS DOWN THE PHONE. SHE HEARS A VOICE)

34.	CHUTKI	May I come in, doctor?
35.	LADY DOCTOR	If it's important, please come in. If it's not, please don't.

(CHUTKI STOPS AT THE DOOR. SHE IS HOLDING A LUNCH BOX)

36. CHUTKI   My sister came here for admission, I have brought food for her.

37. LADY DOCTOR   Ask the nurse, or look in the ward to find her.

38. CHUTKI   She is not there. The nurse said my sister might be with you.

39. LADY DOCTOR   So look around. Do you see anybody?

40. CHUTKI   Thanks, doctor. Despite your headache you heard me out.

41. LADY DOCTOR   (BECKONS TO CHUTKI) Come here, what is your name?

42. CHUTKI   At home I am Chutki, in school I am Priti.

43. LADY DOCTOR   In the hospital?

44. CHUTKI   In the hospital it will be later—Dr Miss Priti.

45. LADY DOCTOR   Half of it is true even now. Miss Priti, does your sister have three daughters, and is your brother-in-law slightly bald?

46. CHUTKI   Yes!

47. LADY DOCTOR   They just left. If you run, you might catch them.

48. CHUTKI   My Jeejaji is a mechanic. He had somebody's car. I cannot run and catch them.

49. LADY DOCTOR   (REACHES FOR THE TELEPHONE) O.K. bye-bye, Miss Priti, I have to work now.

50. CHUTKI   (AS SHE LEAVES) Please don't work so hard at a stretch. My mother does the same, and she often gets these terrible headaches. Then when I oil her hair, she feels better. You also get you your hair oiled by your daughter when you reach home. O.K. bye, Dr Zahir.

(CHUTKI IS LEAVING WHEN DR ZAHIR'S HUSBAND, HASAN ZAHIR, WALKS IN).

51. HASAN ZAHIR   Hello, Dr Zahir.

52. LADY DOCTOR   (IN A DEAD VOICE) Hello, Professor Zahir.

(FADE OUT)

ACT THREE

INT. THE ZAHIR HOME—NIGHT

(LADY DOCTOR IS WEARING A NIGHTGOWN, AND IS BRUSHING HER HAIR. ZAHIR PUTS AWAY HIS BOOKS, AND COMES AND SITS NEXT TO HIS WIFE ON THE BED)

1. HASAN ZAHIR — You look very gloomy. What is the matter? Did you have another tiring shift in the hospital? Did that put you off?

2. LADY DOCTOR — (STRUGGLING WITH HER HAIR) I hate it, and I hate myself for hating it.

(ZAHIR PUTS HIS ARMS AROUND HIS WIFE)

3. HASAN ZAHIR — Tell me, what is it you hate? If there is something you hate, why hate yourself because of it, Aparna?

4. LADY DOCTOR — I hate the maternity hospital ward, where I have to go every day. I am a mother-child lady doctor, who doesn't have a child. I hate this contradiction.

5. HASAN ZAHIR — Aparna, doctors and teachers have a family that extends beyond their house. You are a medical doctor, and I am a university professor, we have countless children.

6. LADY DOCTOR — Did I ask you to come here and cheer me? Am I a kid?

7. HASAN ZAHIR — Look, Aparna. It was your decision that we will not adopt a child. We had agreed that we will help poor, deprived children. The kids whom we help, are they not our kids? Only today I met Seem Singh, who used to work at the small restaurant at the street corner. Remember we paid his tuition and examination fees. He is now working in a firm at Nehru Place. He was saying that he will come visit his mother this Sunday.

8. LADY DOCTOR — His calling me mother does not make me a mother. He is coming on Sunday, why isn't he here with me now?

9. HASAN ZAHIR — You haven't adopted him. Why should he be here?

10. LADY DOCTOR — An adopted child is not one's own.

11. HASAN ZAHIR — (TAKES A DEEP BREATH)

If someone is unable to have a child, and, in principle, does not want to adopt a child, and still complains about not having a child in the house, this is not fair.

12. LADY DOCTOR   Hasan, why don't you say clearly that, Aparna, you are a woman, you are a fool, and you are irrational. Yes, Hasan, I am irrational. There are times I wonder, if electronic goods can become all right after banging them hard, why can't my uterus become all right that way?

(LADY DOCTOR CLENCHES HER FIST AND MOVES IT TOWARDS HER BELLY. HASAN BLOCKS HER HAND. TAKES HER TO BED AND MAKES HER LIE DOWN)

13. HASAN ZAHIR   Relax!

(LADY DOCTOR RISES SUDDENLY FROM THE BED)

14. LADY DOCTOR   No I won't. If you heard the noise in a maternity ward, and returned to the quiet of this flat, even you would be unable to relax.

15. HASAN ZAHIR   (BRINGS HER A SEDATIVE)

This way you would increase your blood pressure. Take this medicine and go to sleep. You will feel better tomorrow.

16. LADY DOCTOR   I am the doctor, not you.

17. HASAN ZAHIR   Listen, Aparna....

18. LADY DOCTOR   I shouldn't behave like a child, isn't that what you want to say? Why are you so wise? Why are you so mature, so patient, so serious? Why doesn't pain affect you? Why don't you get angry? Or do you hide it from your wife? Sometimes you must yell, sometimes you must cry. At least some times you should be sorrowful that you don't have a child. Maybe that's the reason you have made me your little child. And, Hasan, you never give me the privilege to ever treat you as my child.

(SHE WEEPS AT HER HUSBAND'S SHOULDER. ZAHIR COMFORTS HER. SHE TAKES THE MEDICINE THAT ZAHIR BROUGHT TO HER, AND SITS NEXT TO HIM).

Today I had another splitting headache.

19. HASAN ZAHIR   Did you take any medicine at that time?

20. LADY DOCTOR   No. Listen, Hasan, a girl came to the ward looking for her sister. She was saying that her mother also has these headaches, and she oils her hair to comfort her. She asked me to get back home and get my hair oiled by my daughter.

(HASAN GETS A BOTTLE OF OIL)

21. HASAN ZAHIR   Can I be your little daughter, Doctor Zahir??

(FADE OUT)

END OF EPISODE

6

GUIDELINES FOR
SCRIPT PRESENTATION AND REVIEW

Photograph by Harvey Nelson

All scripts need to be carefully reviewed to ensure quality and accuracy.

THE IMPORTANCE OF CORRECT PAGE LAYOUT

In order that everyone who will use the script can refer to it easily and accurately, the script should be presented in a standard format. Major film directors, such as those who work for Bollywood and Hollywood, have their own demands for script layout, using very specific line measurements, fonts and formats. For general script presentation, however, the typical techniques demonstrated in the script extract in this chapter are adequate. The standard presentation requirements are:

Page header

The title of the drama is the first thing on the page, usually given in capital (uppercase) letters and underlined. Under that is presented the number and title of the episode (if a serial drama is being used). Under that comes the name of the author.

Page numbering

Every page in the script should be clearly numbered. Some directors prefer to have the pages numbered at the bottom; others prefer the numbering to be in the upper right hand corner. Similarly, some directors like a numbering system that gives the number of the current page together with the total number of pages in the complete script (e.g., **4 of 44**). This helps ensure that everyone using the script knows exactly how many pages they should have in order to have a complete script.

Scene numbering and setting

The scene number is placed on the left-hand side of the page in capital (uppercase) letters. In addition to the number of the scene, the location is given as well, providing three vital pieces of information:

INTERIOR or EXTERIOR
ACTUAL LOCATION (e.g., BY THE RIVER)
TIME—in terms of "day" or "night"

Description of action

Each action is itemized. Details about action start at the left-hand margin in lower case letters. A double space is left between the scene setting and the action description. A double space is left between the description of action and the lines of dialogue.

Dialogue

The name of the character speaking is given in capital (uppercase) letters in the middle of the page. The actual words to be spoken are printed UNDER the name and are presented in short lines of no more than 40 characters (including spaces). Many writers and directors prefer pica type, which they find easier to read than elite. The reason for this presentation of the dialogue in short lines is to create a script where one page equals one minute of film. All dialogue lines should be double spaced.

Simultaneous action

If the actor is required to make some action (such as shaking hands) while speaking, the writer's instructions for this action are given in parentheses immediately following the character's name.
For example:
CHARLIE (extending his hand)
You are welcome to our house, madam.
We hope you will be very happy here.

Page ending

It is better to avoid dividing an actor's dialogue (speech) between one page and the next—unless it is unusually long. It is much easier for anyone using the script—actor, director, continuity person—if the dialogue is not broken at the end of the page.

CAMERA TERMINOLOGY

In creating a film script, the writer usually does not indicate what the camera angles and shots should be, except in cases where these are vitally important to the interpretation of a scene. When writing an Entertainment–Education television script, however, the writer might need to indicate certain camera shots in order to ensure message accuracy or emphasis. Standard language should be used for these directions so that everyone using the script has the same understanding of what is required. The following is a list of words and phrases that are commonly used for camera directions or suggestions included in the script by the writer or added to the script by the director while preparing for production.

Camera Movements

Boom/Crane
Camera physically moves vertically (up or down).

Jib
Camera moves in combinations of tracking and booming in a single shot.

Pan
Camera swings left or right from a fixed position.

Tilt
Camera swings up and down from a fixed position.

Track/Dolly
Camera physically moves horizontally (left, right, forward or backward), usually on a special metal track.

Zoom
Looks like a camera movement, but actually it is an optical effect generated by a zoom lens mounted on the camera, usually a camera in a fixed position. A "Zoom In" enlarges the subject in the frame. A "Zoom Out" shrinks the subject in the frame.

Descriptive Camera Shots

Close up
This shows the head of a person.

Extreme close up
This shows part of the body (eye, nose, hand, etc.)

Mid shot
This shows from hip to head of a person.

Wide shot
Takes in the entire subject whether it is a landscape, homestead, room or person. A "wide shot" of a person will reveal the full body of a person.

Narrative Terminology for the Camera

Camera finds
The camera moves in on a particular spot on the general picture. This can be used, for example, when a character is looking for something in a scene, or when a character's attention is drawn to a particular object in the scene.

Cut to
This indicates the move from one scene to another. Since "cutting" from one scene to another is virtually automatic in the film and television business, it is not necessary to state this in the script, unless the writer wants to stress that a quick cut is needed for special effect.

Enter frame left or right
An indication that someone or something comes into the camera's scope. A person can be required to "walk into frame" or a vehicle, such as a taxi, can for example, "drive slowly into frame." If it is important that the entrance starts on a particular side of the set, then the "left" or "right" direction is added.

Establishing shot
Usually a wide shot that gives the audience a clear sense of the location where the scene is going to take place.

Hold
The camera "holds" on a particular scene or action rather longer than is usually necessary. This is done for purposes of emphasis or effect, and can be important for message emphasis.

Insert or cut-away
A close-up still shot that is "inserted" into the film during the editing.
For example:
INSERT: CLOSE UP OF MAP SHOWING LOCATION OF BRIDGE.

Montage or series of cuts

A series of shots that can be used, perhaps, in response to a main shot. For example, a series of cuts of faces in a crowd can be used to show a variety of responses to the words of a speaker on a stage or podium.

P.O.V: Point of view

The camera sees from the point of view of one of the characters. For example, P.O.V. LION. This shot would show how the lion viewed a camper. On the other hand, a P.O.V. CAMPER shot could be enhanced by the uneven movement of the handheld camera (shaking due to his/her close proximity to the lion).

Pull back to reveal

The camera moves slowly back from a close-up to a wide shot. This also can be used to show the proximity of one person or object to another, or to show the full extent of a location in which a person or object is located.
For example:
PULL BACK TO REVEAL THAT CHILD IS ON A HIGH BRIDGE CROSSING A BUSY FREEWAY.
Note: This shot would be difficult to achieve smoothly with a handheld camera, unless the camera is firmly anchored in a sling or on a shoulder.

Reverse angle

The camera takes a position that is directly opposite the previous "angle."
For example:
One shot may show the freeway and the traffic from the angle of the child on the bridge. The reverse angle would show the child on the bridge as seen from the position of a driver on the freeway.

Stock shot (stock footage)

Footage that has been shot on a previous occasion and kept to be used on other occasions. Stock footage can be used when the film calls for something that it is impossible or very difficult to shoot as required.
For example, if the script calls for an avalanche or a train wreck, it is undoubtedly easier to use stock footage for this than to set up a real avalanche or train wreck just for the film. Stock footage, however, should be used sparingly. Very often the color or quality of the stock footage does not match comfortably with what is being shot. Poor quality stock footage can detract from the quality of the production.

Tracking or panning shot

The camera moves along with a character or an object that is moving in the scene.

Two shot

The camera covers two people in the same shot. Similarly a **three shot** or even **four shot** requires that the camera covers the stated number of people in the one frame. The placing of two or more people in the same frame requires care so that they look natural, even though they must be closer together than is natural. Similarly, the angle must be correct so that audience attention is drawn to the main character in the group.

Various cuts/angles

This direction is used when it is important to see a scene or a person or an action from a variety of perspectives.

For example, if a speaker on a podium is suddenly shot dead, the script might call for "various angles." This might show reactions from various people in different parts of the hall. At the same time, the "various angles" will suggest to the audience that the shot could have come from a wide variety of places and that locating the killer is going to be a challenging task.

VISUAL EFFECTS

Visual effects are usually generated during the editing process, but can be indicated in the script for narrative purposes.

Dissolve or mix

The picture on screen fades out as a new picture fades in under it.

For example, when moving from one time period to another.

Fade in

The screen begins as a blank and then the picture appears. The appearance can be immediate or gradual. The fade in from black to picture is common at the beginning of many films or television programs.

Fade out

The picture on the screen gradually disappears. This technique is sometimes used at the end of a scene or an act, or the end of a drama. The fade out should be used sparingly and, like the dissolve, should not be relied upon to hide shortcomings in the continuity of the footage that has been shot.

Freeze frame

When a moving subject is stopped in mid motion and held on a still or "frozen" frame.

NARRATIVE DEVICES

Flashback

This is a story device rather than a camera technique. It involves including a scene that takes the viewers back into something that happened earlier in the life of one of the characters. There are occasions when flashbacks can be effective, but flashbacks are easily overused and therefore, it is better—at least for the inexperienced writer or director—not to rely on them.

Dream sequences

Much like flashbacks, dream sequences can be difficult to do convincingly. They should be avoided unless it is absolutely essential to the story that a character's dream be revealed to the audience.

Usually, the dream begins with a close up of the character's face. The shot then fades and perhaps becomes "misty". For a second or two, the screen is a blur, and then the action of the dream begins. To assist the audience in recognizing this as a dream, the scene is often done in lighter colors or with a slight "mist" over the entire scene.

AUDIO EFFECTS AND TECHNIQUES

The importance of sound in a film or TV drama can be appreciated by just covering the ears during an exciting sequence of a film. Music and effects can transform an ordinary event into an incredibly emotional experience. Writers might want to use sound to enhance the emotional impact of a scene, but should not rely on it to compensate for a badly written or poorly produced scene.

Sound effects (SFX/FX)

Virtually all film and television footage has some sound on it. The **SFX** request is included only when a particular sound must be mixed into the local (or ambient) sound for special effect, or to evoke a response from a character.

For example: The local sound in a scene could be the gentle flowing of a river where someone is fishing. The SFX request could be for A TREE CRASHING NEARBY. The sound occurs off camera but is important in the development of the story.

Voice over

A voice is heard that is not coming from the mouth of any character on the screen. The voice over can be the voice of a narrator and is frequently used in documentary films, or in specific-audience videos, like *Song of Life* described in Chapter 7. Sometimes it is used to introduce the new episode of a serial drama, or it can be used to suggest what a character is thinking to herself or himself. The voice over is difficult to use effectively in places other than the introduction to a serial episode. When it is used as the voice of the narrator in some other part of the serial episodes, it tends to destroy the feeling of "looking in on a real world" that an Entertainment–Education drama should instill in the audience. Similarly, if the voice over is used to represent what a character is thinking, it can be equally disturbing because in real life it is not possible to "hear" what a person is thinking.

Script Layout Sample

The following script extract is from one episode of a six-part television series entitled *Time to Care*. This episode is titled "The Dilemma."

Written by John Riber specifically for audiences in Africa, the script demonstrates correct page presentation, and also shows how a good Entertainment–Education drama episode combines emotion and message.

THE DILEMMA
Episode 5
Writer: John Riber   Page 1 of 7

SCENE 1:

EXT. MARKET. DAY.

(KATO AND JOHN FILL A TATA LORRY WITH THE REMAINS OF THEIR MATOKE* OF THE DAY. MAGEZI, A MIDDLE-AGED MAN WITH A DISTINCT STAMMER, HANDS A WAD OF SHILLINGS (MONEY) TO JOHN)

1. MAGEZI	One, two, three, four, five (beat) one two three four five (beat) that's ten thousand. One two three four five (beat) fifteen thousand.
2. JOHN	But that is too much!

---

*Matoke is a form of bread-like food, made mostly of banana and very commonly used by people in some African countries. The word "Beat" which appears in some lines of dialogue indicates that the artists should PAUSE briefly at this point in the dialogue.

THE DILEMMA
Episode 5
Writer: John Riber

3. MAGEZI	Hey! You country boys don't know what you are worth. I market direct to Kampala and get top Shilling for my vegetables, fresh fruit and grain. Do you have m-m-m-more?
4. KATO	We had a good crop this year.
5. MAGEZI	Well, I will give you similar prices for what you have. Bring everything here tomorrow, about m-m-mid day. You guys, you m-m-m-mustn't underrate yourselves. You work hard for your living and deserve better for it.

(JOHN AND KATO BEAM AND SMILE AS MAGEZI BOARDS HIS LORRY AND PULLS OFF. JOHN COUNTS THE NOTES)

6. JOHN	Five thousand for each bunch! Hey, we have struck gold with this one.
7. KATO	It is too good to be true! But he is right. We don't know our worth. We deserve better for our hard work.
8. JOHN	At these prices we can afford to buy those cattle we always wanted.

SCENE 2:

EXT. KATO'S HOMESTEAD. DAY.

(MIREMBE ATTENDS TO HER SIX MONTH OLD DAUGHTER ANNETTE ON A MAT IN FRONT OF THEIR HOME WHEN KATO ARRIVES FROM THE MARKET CARRYING A PLASTIC BAG OF GOODIES. KATO PICKS UP ANNETTE)

1. KATO	Hello my little darling (looking to Mirembe) and my big darling.

(KATO TAKES A PACKET OF IMPORTED COOKIES FROM THE BAG)

2. KATO	See what I have brought for you?
3. MIREMBE	Kato! We can't afford those?
4. KATO	I had a very good day at the market today! And tomorrow will be even better.

THE DILEMMA
Episode 3
Writer: John Riber   Page 3 of 7

| 5. MIREMBE | Really? Can we afford the baby bed for Annette? |
| 6. KATO | No problem. Come, let's go inside and have some tea (pulling a packet of tea from the bag) I will tell you all about it. |

SCENE 3:

EXT. MARKET. DAY.

(KATO AND JOHN ARE JUST FINISHING LOADING MAGEZI'S LORRY WITH A LARGE QUANTITY OF MATOKE, PINEAPPLES, BANANAS AND BAGS OF GRAIN. KATO JUMPS DOWN FROM THE LORRY. MAGEZI SCRIBBLES ON A SMALL NOTEBOOK AND MUMBLES)

| 1. MAGEZI | ...five sacks m-m-maize at 10,000, 40 pineapples at 1,000, 15 kilos of beans at 1,000. |

(ASIDE, KATO TALKS TO JOHN)

2. KATO	That is it. The entire harvest, except for what we need ourselves.
3. JOHN	Shhhh ... he is concentrating.
4. MAGEZI	OK m-m-m-men. By m-m-my figuring, I owe you 195,000 Shillings. Does that sound right?

(KATO AND JOHN SMILE AT EACH OTHER AND NOD)

| 5. KATO | Yes, yes. That sounds about right. |

(MAGEZI MOVES TO THE PASSENGER SIDE OF THE LORRY AND OPENS THE DOOR AND UNLOCKS A WOODEN BOX ON THE SEAT)

| 6. MAGEZI | Normally I would negotiate a 10 percent discount on such a large am-m-m-mount (beat) but I like you guys, and since we are doing business, I want to give you the advantage. |

(HE TURNS AND LOOKS AT THEM)

| 7. MAGEZI | But let me warn you. Next time I am not going to be so generous. Ha, ha, ha. I am a business m-m-man after all.... |

THE DILEMMA
Episode 3
Writer: John Riber

(MAGEZI HAS OPENED THE WOODEN BOX AND LOOKS IN)

8.	MAGEZI	Oh no! Oh no, no, no. (beat)
9.	KATO	What? What is it?
10.	MAGEZI	My m-m-m-manager deposits all the money on Saturdays, Sunday being a holiday. I don't know how m-m-many times I have told him to be sure to draw m-m-money on m-m-m-Monday mornings, but he often puts it off until m-m-m-mid m-m-m-morning. I'm afraid, gentlemen, I'm short of cash.

(MAGEZI TURNS TO KATO AND JOHN)

(KATO AND JOHN LOOK AT EACH OTHER WITH RAISED EYEBROWS)

11.	MAGEZI	Now listen. There are two things we can do. I can run this load into m-m-my warehouse at Kalerwe and come back straight with all your m-m-m-money.

(KATO AND JOHN LOOK PUZZLED)

12.	MAGEZI	The other is to unload and let me go organize the cash first.

(KATO AND JOHN LOOK EXHAUSTED)

13.	MAGEZI	I know this is my fault. I can organize some of these youngsters here to unload for you (beat) if you think that is best.

(KATO AND JOHN LOOK PUZZLED AGAIN)

14.	KATO	How far is your warehouse?
15.	MAGEZI	It's about 20–30 kilometers. You know Kalerwe m-m-m-market, just before Kampala. I have a warehouse there.

(MAGEZI REACHES FOR HIS WALLET AND TAKES OUT A VISITING CARD)

16.	MAGEZI	Here is my card, my phone and address. See here Stand 41, Kalerwe. (beat) Oh, and look here. I do have some m-m-m-money (beat) not a lot, but here, here, let me give you this 20,000 now. That m-m-m-makes a balance of 175,000?

(KATO NODS IN AGREEMENT. JOHN TAKES THE MONEY. MAGEZI BOARDS HIS LORRY AND STARTS THE ENGINE)

THE DILEMMA
Episode 3
Writer: John Riber

17. MAGEZI   I'll be back. (GLANCING AT HIS WATCH) What time is it now? Two P.M. I will be back before 5 P.M.

(THE LORRY ROARS OFF LEAVING KATO AND JOHN)

18. KATO   Wow. That is a lot of money!

(AS THEY MOVE AWAY, THEY HEAR SHOUTING IN THE DISTANCE. TURNING AROUND, THEY SEE THREE MEN SURROUNDING MAGEZI'S LORRY AS IT PULLS ON TO THE HIGHWAY. THE LORRY ACCELERATES, SCREECHING THE AIR HORN. THE MEN DIVE TO THE SIDE TO AVOID BEING RUN OVER AS THE LORRY ROARS ONTO AND DOWN THE HIGHWAY)

(KATO AND JOHN RUSH UP TO THE MEN)

19. MAN ONE   Stop. Stop man and give me my money. You're a thief.

20. KATO   What is going on?

21. MAN ONE   That man. Walter He is a thief!

22. KATO   What?

23. MAN ONE   Last year, he took all of our harvest, promised he would be back in two hours with the money, and we never saw him again (as he stands) until today.

24. KATO   But he is not Walter. His name is Magezi.

(KATO NODS)

25. MAN ONE   Oh, M-m-m-Magezi now is he?

(KATO AND JOHN LOOK AT EACH OTHER HORRIFIED)

SCENE 4:

EXT. MARKET. EVENING.

(KATO AND JOHN SIT WAITING AT THE MARKET. A WELL DRESSED WOMAN PASSES BY)

THE DILEMMA
Episode 3
Writer: John Riber

1.	KATO	Excuse me. What is the time?
2.	WELL-DRESSED WOMAN	Seven o'clock.

(KATO AND JOHN STAND AND WALK AWAY SLOWLY)

3.	JOHN	Don't worry. We'll find him.
4.	KATO	Yes... we will get the bastard.

SCENE 5:

INT. KATO'S LIVING ROOM. NIGHT

(KATO IS SLUMPED OVER HIS UNTOUCHED FOOD, LISTENING TO HIS RADIO. CURRENT NEWS COVERS A BANK ROBBERY. MIREMBE ENTERS FROM THE BEDROOM)

1.	MIREMBE	She is sleeping now. (Excitedly) Did I tell you that she stood by herself today (beat) not for long, but she stood steady, and then sat down. So cute!

(KATO DOES NOT RESPOND)

2.	MIREMBE	What is wrong with you? Why aren't you eating?
3.	KATO	I'm not hungry... just too tired....
4.	MIREMBE	Oh another thing. I think I heard her say "Mama" today. It wasn't really clear, but her mouth was formed into a m-m-m-maaa-maaa.

(KATO LOOKS ANNOYED)

5.	KATO	Enough about Annette!
6.	MIREMBE	Kato? You don't want me to tell you about Annette?

(A LONG PAUSE. KATO TURNS OFF THE RADIO. MIREMBE SITS)

7.	KATO	We had trouble today.

THE DILEMMA
Episode 3
Writer: John Riber   Page 7 of 7

8.   MIREMBE   What trouble?

9.   KATO   The man I told you about yesterday? He took all of our harvest (beat) promised to come back with the money (beat) but didn't return.

10.   MIREMBE   What?

(KATO TURNS TO MIREMBE)

11.   KATO   I think we have lost everything...

12.   MIREMBE   How could you do such a foolish thing? Was it John's idea? The idiot...

13.   KATO   Stop talking like that!

14.   MIREMBE   I ordered the baby bed for Annette today! They are going to deliver it tomorrow.

15.   KATO   Forget the baby bed! We have to think about how we are going to eat!

16.   MIREMBE   But you told me that we would have enough money...

(KATO LOSES HIS TEMPER AND STANDS)

17.   KATO   Shut up woman!!! Don't you understand? We have been cheated of our best harvest ever! We have very little left...

(THE SHOUTING HAS WOKEN THE BABY IN THE NEXT ROOM. MIREMBE, NOW IN TEARS, RUSHES TO THE BEDROOM. KATO WATCHES HER GO AND MARCHES OUT THE FRONT DOOR)

SCENE 6:

INT./EXT. BEER GARDEN. NIGHT.

A relatively quiet week night. A few patrons sit at scattered tables. Kwasa music filters through the air. KIZITO, the proprietor of the beer hall tops up a glass of Waragi on the bar in front of a half-drunk Kato, slumped on a bar stool.

The script continues from here laid out in the same manner.

SCRIPT REVIEW GUIDELINES

Just as every manuscript for a book is edited carefully before publication, and every movie script is thoroughly edited before any production begins, so every script of a behavior change drama should be carefully reviewed and edited before it is shot.

The review team should consist of:

- the program manager
- the director
- two or three content specialists (depending on the number and nature of the topics)
- an Entertainment–Education Drama Specialist (which in some cases might be the program manager)

Initial Review Team Meeting

The program manager should have an initial meeting with the reviewers to share with them the important points of review. Initially reviewers should be reminded that, while they might have exciting story ideas of their own, their job is to ensure the smooth blending of an accurate message and an appropriate story. They should refrain from suggesting changes in the storyline unless they are absolutely essential. In this initial review team meeting, the program manager should also remind the team that television Entertainment–Education dramas are designed:

- to encourage the general public to make beneficial changes in personal behavior and in social norms.
- to contain a strong **main story plot** that will attract and hold the attention of the audience by engaging their emotions. One of the main message topics will be woven into this plot.
- to create three or four subplots (in the case of serial drama); into each of which will be woven ONE of the message topics.

Messages to be included in the drama serial are specified in the design document. It is essential that both writers and reviewers abide by the contents of the design document for every episode. Reviewers should note that the messages do not have to be given in exactly the same words as are used in the design document. The wording will undoubtedly be changed as writers "translate" them into the natural dialogue of the various characters. The important point is that the contents of the message must be correct and understandable to the audience. Messages in the Design Document and in the episodes should be guided by the 7Cs of message presentation (see Box 3.1 on page 67).

Purpose of the Drama

Reviewers should be reminded that it is **impossible** for a television or film audience to take in and remember a lot of specific details from one drama episode or one film. The main **purposes** of the drama, therefore, are:

- To make the audience **aware** of the recommended behavior change and its advantages. Giving too much precise message tends to turn the audience away from, rather than attract them to the behavior change.
- To **encourage** the audience to seek further information (and, where necessary, counseling) from the most appropriate local source.
- **To motivate** the audience to want to find out more about the behavior change in the hope that they will be willing to adopt it and advocate it to others.
- **To model** the appropriate behavior as necessary.

The **purpose** is NOT to provide the audience with every detail of the topic.

Message Location in Episode

In a drama serial, each episode is made up of several **scenes**. Each scene usually continues the story of one plot (either the main plot or one of the subplots), although sometimes there can be two or more scenes devoted to one plot in one episode.

This division of the episode into several scenes means that the message will appear in one—or at the most—two scenes of any episode. Usually, the message should NOT appear in every scene if the drama is to be successful.

The message should NOT appear in the very first scene of a serial drama for the general public. Sometimes viewers do not turn on the television at precisely the right time, so the first scene should move the story forward without containing any specific message. It is generally most successful if the message comes in the **middle** of the episode.

Natural Message Presentation

As much as possible, the message should come into the story in a totally **natural** way. It should not be forced upon the audience like a lecture. There can be—**in, or at the end**

of, every episode—some mention of where the audience can obtain further information about the topic. This might be brought in quite naturally in the characters' dialogue or it can be brought in during the standard closing announcement.

Message Summary

It can be helpful for an announcer to remind the audience **briefly** of the message and the benefits of the recommended behavior change, at the end of the episode. A standard **Closing Announcement** can be used to remind the audience where they can obtain further information on the topic. This announcement can be read as the closing credits are being displayed at the end of the film or episode or shown in advance of the closing credits.

For example:

ANNOUNCER: You have been watching *Time to Remember*. Don't forget to tune in again next week for the next exciting episode of our story. And also don't forget that if you would like further information about any of the important health (or other) messages you heard today, please get in touch with _____ (Name the appropriate organization).

Review Steps

Script review can be done at a regular meeting at which reviewers get together to go through several scripts at one time. If this is not possible because reviewers live far from each other or cannot get together at an appointed time, reviewers should send their comments to the program manager.

In order to provide the most appropriate help in reviewing the scripts, **reviewers should**:

- know what the topic of the episode is and the main points to be covered: check with the design document.
- check the story synopsis to know where the action of the various plots should be.
- check the glossary to be sure that any technical language used in the episode has been correctly explained.

Reviewer's Checklist

With these things in mind, reviewers can check the following points:

1. **Replay:** If there is an Opening Replay reminding audience members of what has happened in the story so far,

   - is it brief?
   - does it remind audience of recent action and message?

2. **Hook:** Does something happen early in the first scene to grab the audience's attention?
3. **Message:** Does the first scene contain message? (It should not)
4. Does the **message** come in naturally and logically?
5. Is the main part of the message towards the middle of the episode? (It should be)
6. Are the main points of the message repeated, subtly, either in the same scene or in another scene?
7. Does the message abide by the **7Cs of message presentation**?
8. Is the message presented as a natural "conversation" or does it seem too much like a lecture?
9. Are the appropriate **emotions** aroused with regard to the message? (See Design Document, point 6)
10. **Characters:** Do main characters have "personality"? Is their personality identifiable through their speech, their actions and/or through what others say about them? Are these same personality characteristics consistent from one episode to another?
11. Are the names of characters used at least once in the scene, but not over-used?
12. Will the audience quickly understand who any new characters are and why they are in the story?
13. **Suspense:** Does each **scene** end on some type of question or suspense (even minimal)?
14. Does the entire episode end on some degree of suspense or question?
15. Does each scene end logically and do the scenes move logically from one to the next—in terms of time, action, message?
16. Does the episode match the **purpose(s)** of the episode in addition to presenting the message? (i.e., does it **demonstrate** some particular behavior if that is called for in the design document?)
17. Does the closing Voice Over announcement (if there is one) make a brief reference to the message as well as encourage listeners to tune in next week?
18. **Plots:** Does the story presentation of each plot suit the chosen audience(s)?
19. Do the plots move forward logically and within an acceptable amount of time? (e.g., the plot should not suddenly leap forward by several years)

20. Are the plots logical? (e.g., just because a man has agreed to have no more than three children, does not mean he will immediately become rich)
21. Do the plots allow for natural **action**, or is there too much static dialogue?
22. Are there limited locations, or are the locations being changed so often that they are confusing for the audience?
23. **Script presentation:** Is the script the right length and are all speeches (dialogues) of acceptable length?
24. Is the script set out in accordance with accepted presentation methods?
25. Are the **Optional Cuts** marked to ensure that if the script has to be cut, the message will not be compromised?

When scripts are being reviewed by several people, it can be time-consuming to go through the scripts and compile all recommended changes. One way to shorten this process is to attach a Review Comment Sheet to each script sent to a reviewer and ask the reviewer to indicate on the sheet the line numbers where changes have been suggested. This Review Comment Sheet can be made along the lines of the sample on the next page.

THE GLORIOUS DAY
Episode 24
Writer: Charlene Gritlo   *Script Review Sheet*

Reviewer Name: _____   **Reviewer Contact Number:** _____

Please write on this page the speech (dialogue) numbers where you recommend changes and the changes you suggest:

General comments: Please also include briefly on the back of this sheet any general comments you have on this episode (negative or positive!)

Please return the script with this cover sheet to: _____

By (date) _____.

7

AUXILIARIES

Enhancing the Message

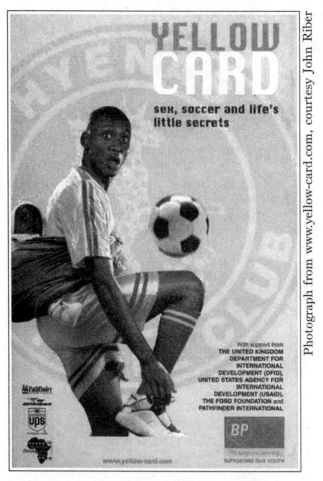

Photograph from www.yellow-card.com, courtesy John Riber

A poster promoting Zimbabwe's popular TV feature film, *Yellow Card*, enhances the message while promoting the drama.

ENHANCING THE MESSAGE: SUPPORT MATERIALS

As noted earlier in this book, there is a universal understanding that one medium alone is usually not enough to bring about long-lasting social change. While the television or film drama might be the primary attraction, it is wise to support this with other media products or with discussion groups or community activities that will remind viewers of the messages and encourage them to learn more.

Print materials are effective only if the audience is literate and the type of print material is appropriate to their interests. Many young people, for example, are not attracted to serious-looking heavy books. They will, however, pick up attractive, colorful leaflets, comics or slim books that will give them quick and easy-to-read information.

The exact type of supplementary materials that should be designed to go with the TV or film project should be decided during the design workshop and developed in time to be available when the drama is being shown to the public.

Literacy Support

In some countries where the literacy level is low (particularly among women), it has been found valuable to develop a literacy program that goes along with the TV drama. Viewers meet together to watch the episodes and then carry out exercises in a literacy workbook that encourages them to answer simple questions about the story or the message or to comment—in writing—on pictures in the book. The stimulation of the drama has been found to be an excellent way of encouraging viewers to learn to read, and—at the same time—to learn about the important messages.

THE FACT PACK

As well as support materials that accompany the drama, it is also possible to enhance the message in other ways. One method is the Fact Pack. Some social development messages are rather too lengthy or too detailed to fit comfortably into an episode of a drama serial. Similarly, the message might be too complex for an audience to recall clearly after viewing one episode of a serial drama. In cases like this, it is possible to enhance the message by the use of a fact pack at the end of each episode.

Typically, the fact pack comes right after the closing scene of the episode and is presented by one of the main message characters of the drama. The Fact Pack is usually only 2–3 minutes long. Briefly, but clearly, it reminds the audience of the important message(s) in the episode.

If a quiz or competition is to be used with each episode, this should be given after the fact pack. Placing the quiz after the fact pack helps to ensure that the audience will pay attention to the important information. They quickly learn that they must stay tuned to the end of the program if they want to have a chance of winning a prize, and that it is highly likely that the information they will need to answer the quiz question will be included in the fact pack.

The following fact pack example is from a Bangladesh TV serial drama, *Ei Megh, Ei Roudro* ("Now Clouds, Now Sunshine") written by Humayen Ahmed.

FACT PACK AND QUIZ: EI MEGH, EI ROUDRO
Episode 11
Time: 3 minutes

The final scene of the episode fades out.

Scene. Village roadside. Day. The doctor is sitting outside his home. Camera is CU on doctor.

1. DOCTOR   So, dear friends, we have learned that Suleman's wife is pregnant. That is good news. It's important that Suleman looks after his wife very well during this time.

(CLOSE SHOT. CAMERA VERY SLOWLY ZOOMS OUT. THE DOCTOR IS TALKING. FADE TO A COLLAGE OF THE VARIOUS POINTS THE DOCTOR IS DISCUSSING)

2. DOCTOR   In today's Health Talk, we will remind ourselves of the health of a pregnant woman. Special care is very important for all pregnant women, because during any pregnancy the lives of both the mother and her unborn baby can be at risk. So, during this period, the pregnant woman must not do any strenuous work and she must eat healthy food like fish, meat, egg, milk, pulses, vegetables, fruits, etc. She should be encouraged to rest for at least one hour during the day, as well as for 8 hours at night.

She has to maintain peace of mind and good health and personal hygiene. And of course, as Suleman now knows, it is essential for the pregnant woman to get support from her husband and every family member.

Oh yes, and she must go for regular check-ups, TT injection, and advice as needed. The husband and family must be sure she is taken to the Smiling Sun Family Health Clinics as instructed by the Health Worker.

(CLOSE SHOT OF DOCTOR. AND THEN MONTAGE OF SMILING SUN CLINIC AS HE GIVES THE ANSWER TO LAST WEEK'S QUIZ)

3. DOCTOR   Oh, but I see that now it's QUIZ time. Let me give you the answer to last week's quiz. The question was, "Where can mothers and fathers and other family members go for advice on feeding their children properly?" The answer, of course, is: "Smiling Sun Family Health Clinics."

(CLOSE UP OF DOCTOR)

4. DOCTOR   And here's this week's quiz question: "What are three things a family must do to take proper care of a pregnant woman?" I repeat: "What are three things a family must do to take care of a pregnant woman?"

So, send your answers to our address and you just might be one of our lucky prize winners. *(The doctor then reads out the address which is also shown on the screen)*

5. DOCTOR   I'll see you next week when we return to our story.

Roll Credits.

VIDEOS FOR A SPECIFIC AUDIENCE

While film and television programs can be an excellent way of motivating behavior change in the general public, there are times when there is more benefit to be gained from creating video programs that will not be shown publicly but will be created for and shown to a restricted audience with planned facilitated discussion.

Know Yourself is a project in Bangladesh designed to use video presentations in adolescent discussion groups to encourage and help young people to learn more about the bodily and psychological changes they go through during puberty; how to protect themselves and others from HIV and AIDS and other Sexually Transmitted Infections; what young married couples need to know about planning their family and preventing unplanned pregnancy. As in many countries, the culture of Bangladesh traditionally has not encouraged any teaching of or even discussion of sexual development for adolescents. Even parents are not in the habit of talking to their children about the changes they will undergo as they move from childhood to adulthood. Ignorance of the facts of bodily and emotional changes has always led to a certain degree of fear and danger for young people.

Throughout the world today with the increase in cinemas and Internet presenting round-the-clock graphic sex scenes, and with the HIV and AIDS pandemic putting young lives at increased risk, there is an urgent need to provide young people with knowledge and skills and motivate them to be responsible so that they can protect themselves and others from unwanted pregnancy and disease.

The *Know Yourself* project was designed with adolescent input at every stage of development and production. The basis of the video project was a series of life-skills workshops attended by a number of adolescents from differing social structures. During the workshops, young people shared their thoughts and questions about reproductive health issues, engaged in role playing, and took part in other activities. A major advantage of engaging adolescents in the creation of this series was that the videos were able to convey sensitive information in a way that was both interesting and acceptable to adolescents and to the communities in which they live.

A production company filmed these activities as adolescents made spontaneous statements and undertook the role playing they had created. These clips were put into the videos, together with a theme song performed by adolescents, some animated sequences and some spontaneous statements from parents and service providers.

These videos were designed to be used, not on public television, but in schools, adolescent clubs and meeting places where a trained group leader could guide and encourage discussion on the points raised in the videos. Each video has a matching life-skills guidebook to be used by facilitators working with groups of adolescents. The videos were further supported with other print materials in the form of question and answer booklets and comic books, to further enhance young people's knowledge of and comfort with talking about and accepting the changes and responsibilities that come with adolescence.

Although the following program is presented in script format, most of the content of the video programs was not scripted; rather, it was compiled from footage that was taken during the workshops, and from interviews or testimonials from adolescents, their parents and their advisors. The mini-dramas were roughly scripted, as were the scenes with the doctors. A certain amount of ad-libbing took place even in the shooting of these partially scripted scenes.

The major advantage of these videos is that they encourage other young people to recognize the fact that they do have the right to express themselves; to speak out; to ask questions and to be given honest answers that will allow them to understand and accept full responsibility for their behavior as they grow into adults.

KNOW YOURSELF
Program 3: Preventing Risks to Our Future   Page 1 of 11

SCENE 1:

AN ADOLESCENT GIRL AND AN ADOLESCENT BOY ARE SEEN ON A STAGE, SINGING.

1. SINGERS

Listen to me my friend, listen intently.
This is not a fairy tale, this is reality—listen carefully.
As you are growing, your body is changing
Some new feelings, new emotions are emerging.
Boys are attracted to girls.
Girls like to tremble at the touch of boys.
But this is not the right time, so let's not have physical relationships.

SCENE 2:

DAY. AT WORKSHOP FOR ADOLESCENTS.

YOUNG PEOPLE ARE ENGAGED IN VARIOUS ACTIVITIES: PHYSICAL EXERCISE; DRAWING, WRITING DRAMAS, ETC.

1. ADOLESCENT MALE (V.O.)

We, a group of adolescent boys and girls, were involved in a four-day workshop. We discussed various possible obstacles to our future plans including teenage pregnancy, HIV/AIDS and other sexually transmitted infections, as well as drug abuse. This video is the result of our discussions on these issues and includes a two-part mini-drama that we developed during the workshop. The opinions of parents and health workers have also been included. The workshop was so much fun. We participated with enthusiasm.

SCENE 3:

AN ADOLESCENT GIRL IS SEEN SEATED AND ADDRESSING THE CAMERA.

1. ADOLESCENT GIRL	When I choose a friend, I will have to decide whether the boy loves me with his heart or only with his body. Whether it is a temporary attraction or if he wants me in his life. Love is natural, holding hands is also natural. But we don't need to kiss because this can lead to touching and sexual relationships.

SCENE 4:

EVENING.

MINI DRAMA. AN ADOLESCENT MALE, RAFIQUE, IS SITTING ALONE. ANOTHER ADOLESCENT MALE, MIZAN, COMES IN AND SPEAKS TO HIM.

1. MIZAN	How are you Rafique?
2. RAFIQUE	Fine, how are you?
3. MIZAN	Well. Why are you sitting here alone?
4. RAFIQUE	Ripa comes home from college this way and I want to talk to her. Why don't you stay too?
5. MIZAN	No, I can't stay.
6. RAFIQUE	Why?
7. MIZAN	There's nobody at home.
8. RAFIQUE	What do you mean?
9. MIZAN	My parents are at my grandmother's.
10. RAFIQUE	Really?
11. MIZAN	Yes.
12. RAFIQUE	Can I bring Ripa to your house?
13. MIZAN	Okay.

KNOW YOURSELF
Program 3: Preventing Risks to Our Future   Page 3 of 11

14. RAFIQUE   Will there be any problem?

15. MIZAN   What problem could there be?

   (RIPA COMES IN FROM ONE SIDE)

16. RAFIQUE   Then you go, we'll come and join you soon.

   (MIZAN GOES OUT)

17. RAFIQUE   How are you Ripa?

18. RIPA   Fine, how are you?

19. RAFIQUE   Well. Take a seat. I want to discuss something with you.

20. RIPA   Quickly, everyone will worry at home. Why do we have to discuss here?

21. RAFIQUE   Mizan's house is empty. Let's go there.

22. RIPA   No, I won't go to an empty house.

23. RAFIQUE   Don't you trust me?

24. RIPA   Why talk about trust and distrust? You know I love you and you love me.

25. RAFIQUE   So why don't you come with me?

26. RIPA   Our relationship would be destroyed. I don't want a sexual relationship with you.

27. RAFIQUE   You won't go?

28. RIPA   No.

SCENE 5:

ADOLESCENT MALE "TESTIMONIAL".

   MALE   Nowadays, adolescents sometimes get into sexual relationships. They're attracted to the opposite sex because of physical urges. If I love a girl and tell her that if we don't have sex our relationship is over, she'll agree to have sex if she doesn't want to end the relationship. These days, many boys satisfy their sexual urges by visiting certain places and many of the girls in those places are adolescents themselves. Because of social and financial reasons, they're in this kind of work. And boys visit them mostly due to peer pressure.

SCENE 6:
DAY.

WORKSHOP. ADOLESCENTS ARE AGAIN ENGAGED IN VARIOUS ACTIVITIES.

FEMALE (V.O)   Adolescents sometimes engage in behavior that puts them at great risk of premature pregnancy and sexually transmitted diseases. We discussed these issues at length during the workshop. We can avoid risky behavior through correct knowledge. That's why we told our facilitator we want to learn more about these diseases and how they spread.

SCENE 7:
SINGERS ON STAGE

SINGERS   You are so young, there's still so much to learn.
When you're not ready, sex results in suffering.
You can get HIV/AIDS and other sexually transmitted diseases.
One mistake may cost your life.
So better be careful.
So listen and learn, life is precious.
Listen to me my friend, listen intently.
This is not a fairy tale, this is reality, so listen carefully.

SCENE 8:
DAY. DOCTOR'S OFFICE

DOCTOR TURNS TO CAMERA AND SPEAKS.

DOCTOR   There are many sexually transmitted infections or STIs such as gonorrhea, syphilis, hepatitis B and C, and HIV/AIDS, etc. These diseases are very dangerous. HIV/AIDS is a killer disease because there's no cure or preventive vaccine so far. "HIV" is the name for the virus that causes the "AIDS" disease.

KNOW YOURSELF
Program 3: Preventing Risks to Our Future

A person infected with HIV may look healthy for a long time. However, the virus destroys the body's immune system. The body gradually becomes weaker and one can get many diseases that will result in death.

STIs can spread when an infected person has sexual intercourse with a healthy person. HIV enters the blood and destroys our white blood cells that help us fight diseases.

CUT AWAY TO ANIMATION OF BLOOD CELLS AND HIV IN BLOOD AS DOCTOR CONTINUES TO TALK.

Then, in the infected blood, HIV multiplies, rapidly making billions of copies of itself which spread throughout the body. If someone has an STI, especially syphilis, and then has sex with an HIV-infected person, it is possible that through an open sore, the HIV virus will be passed on. All STIs are a threat to health and create a great threat to life. STIs, including HIV/AIDS, can be prevented in three ways. The first way is to abstain from having sex until one gets married. The second method is to stay faithful to one partner only. However, if someone cannot follow either of these, the only other thing to do is to use condoms correctly every time you have sexual intercourse.

SCENE 9:

ADOLESCENT BOY AND ADOLESCENT GIRL TESTIMONIALS.

ADOLESCENT BOY
Nowadays adolescents in our country, like those in many other countries, are involving themselves in risky behavior. It is better to avoid risky behavior. But if someone, due to peer pressure or some other reasons, gets involved in such behavior, then he must use condoms. Risky behavior can lead to sexually transmitted infections and unwanted pregnancy. In every sexual intercourse, a condom must be used.

ADOLESCENT GIRL
I don't think there should be any kind of physical relationship before marriage. And if people can't control their passions, they must use condoms. If they don't do so, they may get one of several diseases ... for example, syphilis, gonorrhea, AIDS.

KNOW YOURSELF
Program 3: Preventing Risks to Our Future

| ADOLESCENT BOY | If symptoms of STIs are detected or if someone suspects they have an STI, then they must immediately consult a qualified doctor. Even without visible symptoms there may be STIs in the body. In many cases symptoms are not easy to detect by just looking at the person. |

CUT AWAY TO ANIMATION OF BLOOD CELLS AND HIV.

| ADOLESCENT BOY (V.O.) | Having sex without condoms can lead to HIV/AIDS. In addition, the disease can spread if you use injection needles and syringes that have already been used by someone else or through having a blood transfusion that contains infected blood. |

| ADOLESCENT BOY (ON CAMERA) | Drug addiction has bad consequences. For example, those who take pethidine often pass the injection needles from one user to another ... up to five or six users ... even up to 10. We know that if many people use the same needle, HIV can easily spread because at least one of the users might already be infected and that person's blood can be passed through the injection needle. HIV/AIDS and other dangerous diseases like syphilis, hepatitis B and C can spread through an infected syringe or needle. |

CUT TO SHOTS OF ADDICTS AND THEN A MONTAGE OF THE BOY'S LIFE.

Today more of our adolescents are becoming addicted to drugs. Why are they getting addicted? We must try to find the reasons. Some start using drugs because of peer pressure or due to a broken heart. Others do it because it's trendy. I studied up to class 5 in the village. Then I moved to my uncle's in the city. Nearby there is a market. I used to hang around there. Gradually, I made some friends.

At one point, I started smoking. Then, I started taking different kinds of drugs. I used to hang around quite late. Late at night, secretly, I used to take heroin. To support the habit, I stole various things from my uncle's house. I even stole and sold my Aunty's saris and jewelry. Then gradually, my downfall began. At this point, my uncle realized what was going on. He forced me to enter a clinic. There, I had a difficult month. Then I was treated by the doctor, and I recovered.

KNOW YOURSELF

SCENE 10:

DAY. DOCTOR IN HIS OFFICE.

DOCTOR	In adolescence, many physical and mental changes happen. Too often young people do not know about these changes in advance. If adolescents approach their parents with any questions or physical or mental problems, then parents must be understanding and help their young people to find solutions to their problems.

SCENE 11:

A GROUP OF TEENAGERS SITTING TOGETHER. THE CAMERA CLOSES IN
ON THE ONE WHO SPEAKS.

ADOLESCENT BOY	Sexual intercourse, sexual diseases and how they spread. We want and need to know about these things. And to talk about these things, we need a good facility. We can't talk about such things with just anyone. If we discuss such issues openly, people will think we are bad. So, we need a facility where we can openly discuss these things and get correct answers. And we don't need to be treated as if we are bad.

SCENE 12:

DAY. DOCTOR'S OFFICE.

MINI DRAMA. WE SEE A DOCTOR TALKING WITH TWO ADOLESCENT BOYS.
ONE BOY IS THERE WITH A PROBLEM; THE OTHER IS THERE TO SUPPORT
HIS FRIEND. THE DOCTOR SHOWS NO INTEREST IN THE BOYS AND SEEMS
EAGER TO GET RID OF THEM.

1. DOCTOR	Assalamu walikum.
2. BOY	Walaikum assalum. Doctor, we'd like to talk to you about something.
3. DOCTOR	But ... how? what are you saying? Go ahead ... I mean ... Why don't you speak clearly?

KNOW YOURSELF

4. BOY	(HESITATINGLY) Doctor, I have sores around my penis. It has become swollen. And ... pus comes out when I urinate. What? What's this?
5. DOCTOR	Stand further away! How old are you two?
6. BOY	Sixteen and seventeen.
7. DOCTOR	Do you have parents?
8. BOTH	Yes.
9. DOCTOR	Are you in school?
10. BOTH	Yes ... we are.
11. DOCTOR	So, what did you do to get this disease?
12. BOY	Well ... I mean...
13. DOCTOR	What do you mean? Tell me how it happened.
14. BOY	Well ... I mean?
15. DOCTOR	What do you mean? Go! Get out of here! Go!

SCENE 13:

PARENT ADDRESSING CAMERA.

PARENT	We visit a health service provider or doctor when we have health problems. A few good words from them and a friendly attitude can make it easier to discuss our problems. And this is especially true for our adolescent children. Let's see the difference.

SCENE 14:

DOCTOR'S OFFICE.

MINI DRAMA. A DIFFERENT DOCTOR WITH A DIFFERENT ATTITUDE TO THE SAME TWO BOYS.

1. BOY	Assalamu walikum, doctor.

KNOW YOURSELF
Program 3: Preventing Risks to Our Future

2. DOCTOR	Walaikum assalum. Please sit down. How are you?
3. BOY	Fine, sir.
4. DOCTOR	What's going on?
5. BOY	Doctor, we would like to learn something from you. Do you have some time?
6. DOCTOR	Yes, of course. It's no problem. What is it?
7. BOY	No... I mean... Won't you be disturbed?
8. DOCTOR	No, why should I? Tell me your problem. Are you uncomfortable asking me about something?
9. BOY	No... I mean... Doctor, what is gonorrhea? ... Oh....
10. DOCTOR	Now I know what you are asking me.It's important for you to know about this. Gonorrhea is a sexually transmitted infection. It spreads from one person to another through sexual intercourse.
11. BOY	Will everyone who has sex get it?
12. DOCTOR	No, it's not like that. Ok, let me explain it to you. The infections which spread through sexual intercourse are called ... sexually transmitted infections. They are gonorrhea, syphilis, HIV/AIDS, and hepatitis B and C.
13. BOY	How would we know if we had any of these infections?
14. DOCTOR	The major symptoms of sexually transmitted infections are: drops of pus from the sexual organ, pain or burning sensation during urination, and sores in and around the sexual organ. If you suspect that you have any of these symptoms, consult a qualified doctor, like me, without delay. Ok, now tell me: Do you suspect that you may have any problem? Don't hesitate. Please share with me.

KNOW YOURSELF
Program 3: Preventing Risks to Our Future

SCENE 15:

COMMENT FROM PARENT—ON CAMERA.

1.	PARENT	In our country, health services for adolescents are totally inadequate. We have centers for children and mothers. For adolescents, we should set up special health centers, where they could freely discuss their concerns in a friendly atmosphere, and could get proper advice for their physical problems. Then it would be very good.

CUT TO ADOLESCENT GIRL.

2.	ADOLESCENT GIRL	At our age, we have many questions. If we could discuss things with our parents or health workers or some adults in a friendly and frank way, it would be good for us. The things we are going through ... those problems, opportunities, good things, should be openly discussed with us.

SCENE 16:

DAY.

WORKSHOP SEQUENCE. ADOLESCENTS ENGAGED IN WORKSHOP ACTIVITIES.

ADOLESCENT GIRL	During the workshop we enjoyed learning many new things. We had discussions regarding our questions about adolescent life. And the book that was shared with us was very helpful too. This book, written on the basis of questions and answers of adolescents helped us to learn many important facts. Discussions during the workshop helped clear our misconceptions on many matters. Many people believe that it is inappropriate for adolescents to learn about sexual relationships, behavior and diseases.
	Through this workshop and after knowing all these issues we feel safer and more aware. We believe that having the knowledge and skills on these issues will help us to make right choices in the future.

KNOW YOURSELF

SCENE 17:

THE SINGERS APPEAR ON STAGE TO END THE VIDEO.

SINGERS   Your life's journey has just begun, you have many a mile to go.
To live your life, you need the right knowledge.
Short-lived bliss vanishes, but the pain remains.
For mistakes, you may have to pay with your life.
So, not in errors, not in mistakes, live your life in the right way.
Listen to me my friend, listen intently.
This is not a fairy tale. This is reality. Listen carefully.

Roll credits to end.

PART 4

For the Producer, Director, and Filmmaker

8

GUIDELINES FOR PRE-PRODUCTION
Needs, Budgets, and Contracts

Photograph by John Riber

Locations must be carefully chosen to suit both the story and the audience.

PRE-PRODUCTION IS PLANNING

Pre-production is the period of planning after the script is approved and before shooting begins. The more time devoted to pre-production, the better are the chances of the film or serial drama being of good quality. During pre-production, the program manager and the director work closely together to ensure quality, accuracy, timeliness and budget details. Every creative decision that the director considers will have logistical, financial, and quality implications. Similarly, all financial and logistical decisions the program manager considers could have an impact on creative possibilities. Complete co-operation is essential, therefore, between program manager and director in all pre-production decisions.

PRE-PRODUCTION ACTIVITIES

The first aim of the pre-production period is the finalization of the budget and the contracts. Achieving this end requires a number of interim steps:

- Script breakdown
- Selecting the production crew

- Auditioning and selecting the actors
- Listing and locating needed props
- Determining logistical needs and arrangements
- Identifying and scheduling locations
- Ensuring availability of shooting equipment, studio and post-production needs

Script Breakdown

Script breakdown clarifies and notes the following points of the drama:

- The number of different days the story involves (this knowledge is needed to determine such matters as change of costumes for actors)
- The number and type of locations needed
- The number of scenes that must be shot in daylight
- The number of scenes that must be shot at night (or in early morning or late afternoon)
- The number and type of characters (those with speaking roles) required
- The number of extras (those without speaking roles) required
- The clothes and other props each character will require in each scene. The word "props" is short for the word "properties." Properties are things—other than costumes or scenery—that are used in dramatic production.

Box 8.1

SCRIPT BREAKDOWN

- different days in the drama
- different locations
- scenes to be shot during the day
- scenes to be shot at night
- characters and type of actors needed

From these script breakdown details the producer and director can make logistical and management decisions on matters like:

- the exact locations where the film will be shot and the cost of location hiring (if any)
- the schedule for the shooting crew and actors on each location
- transport needed for all personnel to and from the locations

- catering needs for all personnel during shooting accommodation, where necessary, at distant locations

Script breakdown details

For scheduling purposes, script pages are broken into eighths. The shortest fraction of a page a scene can cover is 1/8. Scenes must be carefully numbered and the scene list must identify the following factors that assist in determining the order in which scenes will be shot:

Time of day or night

If the drama calls for the shooting of several scenes at night, it is possible to arrange for night shoots, working from 6 P.M. to 6 A.M. Alternatively, split schedule shooting days can be arranged that can take advantage of both daylight and darkness. The split schedule allows for shooting of daylight scenes during the afternoon and night scenes after dark. Some night-time interior scenes can be shot during the day by blacking out doors and windows. This can be done with black plastic sheeting hung over the outside of the windows. Exterior night scenes, on the other hand, must be scheduled for after-dark shooting.

Exterior or interior

Setting up the necessary equipment for a shoot in a relatively small interior space (such as a room in a house) is often a time-consuming challenge. It is wise to do all scenes in the same interior location at one time in order to save the expense of moving and re-setting the furniture and the film equipment.

Characters involved

Some films have a few main locations where many scenes are shot involving many different characters. Scheduling must determine the sequence in which the locations are covered and how the people and equipment are moved from one location to the next.

Scene length

Scene length as indicated in pages and eighths of pages.

On the next page, an excerpt from the script breakdown for the drama *A Time to Care* shows how these items can be displayed:

SCRIPT BREAKDOWN
A TIME TO CARE

KANSANGATI LOCATIONS

EXTERIOR, MARKET	time	pages	**total 9,3/8 pages**
Sc. 1 Ext. Market	day	1,2/8	Kato/John. Magezi
Sc. 3 Ext. Market	day	4,6/8	Kato/John/Magezi/Man 1/Man 2
Sc. 4 Ext. Market	day	3/8	Kato/John/Well-dressed man
Sc. 10F Ext. Market	day	1/8	Kato
Sc. 23A Ext. Market	day	1/8	Kato
Sc. 36 Ext. Market	day	6/8	Kato/John/Kizito
Sc. 37 Ext. Matoke Vendor	day	2	Kato/John/Kizo/Vendor/Stranger

EXTERIOR APPROACHING MARKET			**total 1,1/8 pages**
Sc. 35 Ext. Approaching Market	day	1,1/8	Kato/John

EXTERIOR, KATO'S PLACE			**total 1,1/8 pages**
Sc. 2 Ext. Kato's house	day	7/8	Kato/Mirembe/Annette
Sc. 10A Ext. Kato's house	day	1/8	Kato/Mirembe/Transporters
Sc. 23C Ext. Kato's place	day	1/8	Kato/Mirembe/Annette

EXTERIOR, GARDEN			**total 3,7/8 pages**
Sc. 10B Ext. Garden	day	1/8	Kato
Sc. 11 Ext. Garden	day	1	Kato/John
Sc. 20 Ext. Garden	day	1	Kato/Mirembe/Annette
Sc. 23E Ext. Garden	day	1/8	Kato/Mirembe/Annette
Sc. 23F Ext. Garden bush	day	1/8	Kato
Sc. 24 Ext. Garden	day	1,4/8	Kato/Mirembe/Annette

EXTERIOR/INTERIOR CLINIC			**total 1,3/8 pages**
Sc. 29 Int. Clinic Ward	day	1/8	Kato/Mirembe/Catherine
Sc. 30 Ext. Clinic Corridor	day	1	Kato/Catherine
Sc. 31 Int. Clinic Ward	day	1/8	Kato/Mirembe

EXTERIOR, JOY'S PLACE			**total 3,5/8 pages**
Sc. 22 Ext. Joy's place	day	2,4/8	Mirembe/Joy/Annette
Sc. 26 Ext. Joy's place	day	1,1/8	Mirembe/Joy/Annette

EXTERIOR, JOHN'S PLACE			**total 2,3/8 pages**
Sc. 19 Ext. John's place	day	2,3/8	Kato/John

INTERIOR, DRUG STORE			**total 1,4/8 pages**
Sc. 12 Int. Drug Store	day	1,4/8	Kato/Lubega/Joy

Breaking down the script scene by scene this way allows the director to determine exactly how many locations will be needed and to budget for those that will require a hiring fee. Listing the locations also allows the director to determine such things as the amount of time and transport needed to reach any particular location. Based on the script breakdown, the director can advise actors, during the audition process, if it will be necessary for them to be away from home for any period of time. If the script breakdown indicates that there is insufficient budget to cover all these costs, then determinations must be made at this stage with regard to how to adjust the script to fit the budget.

Selecting the Production Crew

Creating film or TV drama requires many people besides the actors. A minimum of 15 people is usually required for the production crew alone and this must be allowed for in the budget. The production crew can be divided into departments, each of which can be responsible for budgeting for and providing its own requirements. These department budgets are incorporated into the main budget as final cost determinations are made. The departments are:

Management department

This consists of the producer and the director. The producer is the ultimate authority on issues involving funding, project policy, and script, production, and editing approval. The director is the filmmaker who is the leader of the production team and the creative authority on location during the filming.

Production department

This department comprises the production manager/coordinator, the continuity manager, and, in some cases, a Message Monitor. The production manager is in charge of all logistics including personnel movements and location arrangements. The continuity manager provides general support for the director, maintains records of scene completion, organizes shooting schedules, movements on the set and smooth transition from one scene to the next. The Message Monitor is an important team member for Entertainment–Education serial dramas, where it is essential that the wording of the messages, and sometimes the setting for and method of the message presentation, is absolutely accurate.

Lighting, sound, and camera department

Those involved in this department are:

- the lighting camera person, who lights the scenes and works with the director to plan shots and also operates the camera;
- the camera assistant, who is responsible for the mechanical operation and maintenance of camera equipment (charging batteries, cleaning lenses, etc.) and

for maintaining records of camera operations and providing general support for the lighting camera person;

- the location sound recordist, who operates the field mixer, controls recording levels, monitors location recording and works with the director and lighting camera person to determine the best microphone positions;
- the boom operator, who swings the microphone boom and gives general support to the sound recordist;
- the gaffer-electrician, who checks power sources, runs cables and sets the lights at the instruction of the lighting camera person; and
- the key grip, who moves camera and lighting equipment.

The wardrobe manager

Responsible for locating and maintaining the costumes (clothes) to be worn by the actors, and for selecting and applying make-up to the actors as needed.

The art and props manager

Responsible for purchasing, hiring or borrowing all "props" (such as furniture, accessories, personal requirements like handbags and books) required in each scene of the drama, and for the general appearance of the sets (e.g., walls painted, grass cut, trees trimmed as required, etc.)

The transport department

Usually has a minimum of three drivers (one for the cast; one for the crew; one for the camera and sound equipment). One of the drivers will have the task of **transport manager** and will work closely with the production manager to coordinate all transport movements. Other drivers can double as production and grip assistants, helping with loading and unloading equipment and running errands and messages.

Auditioning and Selecting Actors

Before the auditioning of actors begins, the director must determine the important attributes of each character in the drama. If the writer has presented detailed character profiles with the script treatment, the director can work from that. If not, the director, while studying the script, should make notes on what to look for in the selection of actors. The following page shows the "Character and Attribute Sheet" for the drama *A Time to Care*.

A TIME TO CARE
CHARACTERS AND ATTRIBUTES

MIREMBE	Rural heroine. Early to mid-20s. Farmer's wife. Primary education. Newly married to Vincent and without children. Strong rural background.
KATO	Rural hero. Irene's husband. Mid to late 20s. Farmer. Limited education. Strong rural background.
CATHERINE	Nurse at Health Center. Late 20s/early 30s. Well-educated and articulate. Modern small-town background.
BIRUNGI	Traditional midwife. Middle-aged or older. Strong rural background.
JOY	Irene's best friend. Late 20s. Secondary education. Married with two children. Middle class. Modern small-town background.
JOHN	Farmer. Irene's brother-in-law. Mid-30s. Limited education. Tired and worn. Strong rural background.
JOSHUA	Sophie's son. Teenage boy. Strong rural background.
ANNETTE	Irene's sister. Late 20s. Tired and worn. Strong rural background.
RECEPTIONIST	Young to middle-aged woman at Health Center.
JANET	Joy's sister at Health Center.
MZEE	Old man at Health Center.
WOMAN	Middle-aged pregnant woman at Health Center.

It is also important to know the number of days each actor will be needed before starting auditions. The director must be able to tell the auditioning actors how many days they will have to devote to the shooting of the drama. The following list shows the amount of time needed by each of the actors in *A Time to Care.*

A TIME TO CARE
BUDGET FOR ARTISTS' TIME NEED ON THE SET

Kato (every day)	10 days
Mirembe	8 days
John	5 days
Joy	4 days
Kizito	4 days
Catherine	3 days
Maria	3 days
Magezi	3 days
Lubega	2 days
Stranger	2 days
Matoke Vendor	2 days
Man 1	2 days
Man 2	2 days
Well-dressed Man	2 days

The budget for artists' time will allow the director to make an accurate determination of what this part of the production will cost. The list of attributes for the leading characters will assist the director in choosing appropriate actors. With these important determinations made, the director can begin to look for, audition, and select the actors who will play the leading parts.

Listing Needed Props

Small items, such as books, money, cups, flowers, indeed anything that can be picked up and used by the actors, are all considered to be "props." Sometimes the needed props can be provided by the actors themselves, but frequently special props are needed that must be located and hired or borrowed for the shoot. Sometimes it is necessary to purchase props, especially if they are to be destroyed or eaten as part of the action of the film. Pre-production preparations must include a full list of all props needed in the entire production so that their purchase or rental can be included in the final budget.

Determining Logistical Needs and Arrangements

The making of a film requires that a number of people (often quite a large number) will be on location at one time. These people must be transported to the location site, and they must be fed during the hours they are on the job. All these costs must be accounted for in the budget. Logistical needs therefore include determining, arranging and budgeting for:

- transport needs
- catering needs
- places for crew and actors to sit while awaiting their turn on camera
- overnight accommodations—where necessary
- medical assistance should it be necessary

Other logistical needs and arrangements might be needed in addition to those listed, depending on the nature of the film.

Identifying and Scheduling Locations

It is not always easy to find locations that exactly match the needs of the script. It can be difficult to locate exactly the right market corner, the appropriate house, the accessible nightclub or hospital that will allow entry to a film crew. Sometimes it is necessary to obtain written permission and perhaps provide payment to use a particular location, such as a temple. Some private property owners require compensation for the use of their property. Some government organizations require compensation for the time spent by staff on government premises who give assistance during shooting. All locations, therefore, must be specifically identified, contracted for (where necessary) and scheduled well before the shoot begins. All key personnel (director, camera director, lighting and sound personnel and in some cases the writer) must know and approve the locations. The program manager should also be acquainted with the chosen locations to be sure that they are appropriate to the messages of the Entertainment–Education drama and to the chosen audience. Determinations of the costs of hiring or using the chosen and approved locations must be included in the final budget.

Shooting Equipment and Post-production Needs

Most production houses or filmmakers do not own all the equipment they need for a production. They hire the equipment as they need it. Equipment hire, therefore, becomes a major part of budget considerations. It is during the pre-production phase that the director must ascertain exactly what on-location equipment will be needed, including cameras, dollies, tracks, sound equipment and lights. Prices for the hire of the equipment must be agreed upon, as must the availability of the equipment on the intended shooting dates.

Prices and availability must also be determined for all studio services, such as picture and sound editing, music, titles, voice-over dubbing, sub-titles, etc.

Budget Finalization

Once all these points have been determined, it is possible to put together final budgets. Where a television or video drama is being used with a social development project, it is typical that a pre-determined budget has been allocated for the event. The actual and final budget, however, can be determined only when the script has been completed, all script requirements have been noted, and the needs of each department determined. In order to be sure that everything has been covered, the budget should be reviewed carefully by the director and the program manager. Sample budgets can be found in Appendix C.

Contract Finalization

The budget and the final contracts are somewhat interdependent and often these two areas of pre-production must be determined at the same time. Once the program manager and the director have completed the script breakdown and are confident that the budget can cover the script needs, they can begin to select the cast and crew and draw up the necessary contracts. Typically, production crews are contracted to work 12 hours a day, six days a week. The cost of hiring production equipment and of logistical support is very high, so the crew needs to make use of every minute of available daylight. Film crews work long, hard days and should be compensated accordingly.

Each person involved in the production must have a written contract specifying the duration of the contract period, the responsibilities of the person named in the contract (including the responsibility to supply and maintain equipment) and the amount and methods of payment. It is often helpful to crew and cast members to be given an initial payment at the time of signing the contract so that they can devote the necessary time to the project without having to undertake other work to tide them over financially until the film is completed.

Contracts must be drawn up for every activity in the production process: equipment, transport, catering, locations, props, wardrobe and make-up, editing, music, cast, crew and anything else that involves money.

Special Contract Clauses

The program manager should consider including special responsibility clauses in some contracts. Such special clauses can be especially helpful in the case of the director and the writer(s). Special clauses might require the signatory to agree

- to abide by the contents of the design document.
- that the program manager/producer is the ultimate authority in all aspects of the project.
- that the final choice of writer will be made only when possible writers have submitted audition scripts written after their attendance at the design workshop. (This clause is always necessary in cases where the suggested writers are unknown to the program manager or where the writers are known but have not previously worked in the Entertainment–Education format.)
- to a penalty for late delivery of scripts. Such a clause is especially helpful in the case of serial writing where episode writing must be completed by the specified date if the time line is to be maintained.

Sample contracts for crew and cast members can be found in Appendix D.

Successful filmmaking requires precise attention to detail. Successful Entertainment–Education television drama serial production puts equal emphasis on the importance of an attention-getting story and accurate and convincing message presentation. The pre-production period is the time in which as many details as possible are examined and finalized. Considerable time, money, and frustration are saved if pre-production is carried out thoroughly and if all areas of pre-production are agreed upon jointly by the program manager and the film director.

Once budgets and contracts have been finalized, or even during their finalization, the director can begin work on the next step: artistic preparation.

9

GUIDELINES FOR PRE-PRODUCTION
Artistic Preparation

Photograph by Harvey Nelson

Some directors create models of required locations to ensure accuracy.

PREPARING FOR THE SHOOT

The **shoot** is the most expensive and intensive period of any film production and must be done as efficiently, but accurately, as possible. It is advisable to complete the entire shoot without interruption. This means that once the shooting schedule has been prepared, it should be followed scrupulously. If production falls behind for any reason, every effort should be made to catch up, even if this means less coverage or combining scenes, or even dropping scenes (or optional cuts) that are not essential to the story and contain no message. Usually, it does not work to plan to take "pick-up" shots at the end of the shoot.* Inevitably, the extra time needed for these shots is not available when the shooting is completed and the resulting gaps in the film can be disastrous at editing time.

A smooth and on-time shoot obviously requires excellent organization and preparation. This preparation involves not only all technical details, but also thorough and careful artistic planning by the director.

VISUALIZATION

The most important aspect of artistic pre-production is the visualization of the script. Visualization means more than just choosing locations that are appropriate and actors who look the part. It also means determining the picture each scene will present to evoke the appropriate response in the audience. Therefore, for each scene, the director must

---

*Pick-up shots are necessary close-ups of objects (such as the page of a book being read by a character) or add-ins such as the view through the window that are not shot while the main action is being filmed.

decide the emotion to be aroused: fear, mystery, love, ignorance, confusion, or any one of hundreds of other possible human feelings. Sometimes the decision about the emotion of a scene is influenced by the behavior change motivation that is needed and by the overall emotion selected by the design team. Decisions about emotional stress will affect not only where and when the scene is shot, but also how it is shot: In a combination of long shots, medium shots and close-ups? From overhead? From a low position, looking up? With a moving camera? In pale light? Moreover, it is important that the visual interpretation of each shot fits harmoniously with the shot before and after it.

Visualization is every bit as important to the success of a drama as is the worded script. Indeed, there are many directors who would argue that visualization is more important than the script. It is certainly of major importance in Entertainment–Education dramas because the visual presentation of the script can have a profound influence on the film's ability to inspire behavior change in the chosen audience.

For example, a filmed drama is unlikely to persuade viewers to give up smoking if every scene is shot in colorful and cheerful close-ups of rich and beautiful people enjoying themselves smoking cigarettes.

Different directors have different ways of assembling their thoughts on visualization of the drama. Some like to do it with written sentences, one sentence describing each shot; others use file cards on which to write a concise statement of each shot; others make detailed shot lists and some prefer to use storyboards, either paper or computer-generated versions.

Storyboards

Storyboards are usually actual hand-drawn pictures (these days many are computer-generated) showing the shots the camera should capture in the scene. These drawings, which might be stick-figure sketches or veritable masterpieces of art work, allow the director to see or to visualize—before any shooting has begun—how the finished scene will look. The pictures are not moving, of course, but they provide an effective "shorthand" view of what the finished scene will present to the audience.

Storyboards can be as simple as file cards with written directions for shooting:

WOMAN WALKING TO MARKET. WE SEE HER FROM BEHIND.	REVERSE ANGLE. WE SEE AGONY ON HER FACE AS SHE STUMBLES AND ALMOST FALLS.

Storyboards can also be presented as stick-figure sketches that give rather more detail than is provided by notes on file cards (see Figure 9.1).

Some of the most famous film directors of the past, like Alfred Hitchcock, required fully detailed storyboards, with accurately drawn pictures of the scene to be shot.

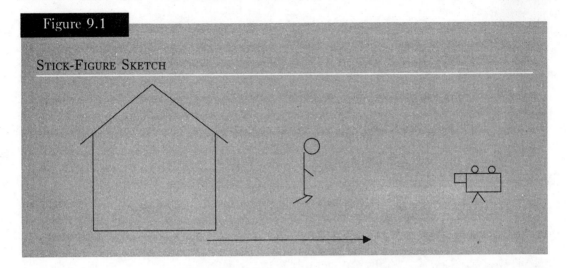

Figure 9.1

STICK-FIGURE SKETCH

The choice of detailed storyboards or written scene descriptions is personal to each film-maker, but the important factor is that each scene should be carefully and completely visualized before the cameras and sound equipment are set up.

Some directors like to prepare actual small models of certain scenes to assist themselves in determining how the right atmosphere can be suggested and the action can best be caught.

The chosen method of visualization really depends on the preference of the director. Many times changes will be made when shooting begins, but the chances of a film being successful are greatly enhanced when the director—perhaps with the help of the camera crew and a graphic artist—takes the time to make careful notes (written or pictorial) on the visualization of each scene. In those scenes where the location is an important part of the message—such as inside a clinic or hospital—it is important to include the Message Monitor in determining how the scene should look.

Once the script has been approved, the director studies it thoroughly to develop the first outlines of how the story will be visualized. Possible locations can be considered at this time and the need for building any special set(s) can be determined. With initial visualization ideas in mind, the director visits each location with the camera and sound crews to map out where the action of each scene will take place and to visualize just how each sequence will be covered. The final visualizations can be recorded in any of the following ways.

Shot Lists

Shot lists can be prepared during the location visits. Even if the coverage changes a little during the actual shoot, it is essential that shot lists are prepared in advance. At the same time as writing the shot lists, the director might make some written notes on the script of each scene to clarify exactly how the scene will be shot. Many directors use lines of different colors on the script to indicate which sections will be covered by which type of shot (yellow = wide shot, pink = mid shot, green = close-up, etc.).

The following samples show—at the bottom of each page—the notes the director made while visualizing one of the scenes in *The Dilemma*. The notes are followed with some shot list samples. A similar set of notes was made for each scene in the film:

SCENE 30:
EXT./INT. DAY. HEALTH CENTER CORRIDOR.

(CATHERINE WALKS KATO DOWN THE CORRIDOR SLOWLY)

SISTER CATHERINE   I'm afraid the baby will not survive.

KATO   She's pregnant?

SISTER CATHERINE   You didn't know?

(KATO SHAKES HIS HEAD)

SISTER CATHERINE   Mirembe has an STI. It has affected her pregnancy. The STI is causing her to miscarry.

KATO   She never complained of any problem.

SISTER CATHERINE   Unlike men, women often do not notice any symptoms with an STI until it is at an advanced stage. That is why it is so important for men to tell their partners when they have an STI ... so both can be treated right away.

(KATO STOPS WALKING)

SISTER CATHERINE   Excuse me, Kato.

(SISTER CATHERINE WALKS DOWN THE CORRIDOR. KATO TURNS SLOWLY AND RETURNS TO THE WARD)

Notes: *This scene will be covered in one telephoto shot. We will record the sound up close and then lay the sound over the best shot we get.*

SCENE 33:

INT. DAY. CATHERINE'S COUNSELING ROOM.

(KATO AND MIREMBE ARE SEATED IN THE COUNSELING ROOM)

SISTER CATHERINE   I will need to see you both again in two weeks, after Mirembe has completed the course, to be sure that the treatment has worked.

(KATO AND MIREMBE NOD IN AGREEMENT)

SISTER CATHERINE   STIs are very dangerous. The STI is what caused your miscarriage. Babies born to mothers with STIs often die soon after birth. Untreated, STIs can also lead to infertility in both men and women.

(KATO GLANCES OVER AT MIREMBE)

KATO   But we want to have more children.

(MIREMBE NODS IN AGREEMENT)

SISTER CATHERINE   The treatment I have given you should clear up the infection.

(SISTER CATHERINE REACHES FOR A STRIP OF CONDOMS)

Notes: *This scene will be filmed in 6 shots:*
Mirembe reaction—full scene
Close-up Catherine—full scene
Wide master shot towards Catherine—full scene
Two shot, Kato over shoulder of Catherine—full scene
Close-up, Kato, full scene
Two shot, Catherine over shoulder of Kato—full scene

The following Shot List is from the film *Caring Completely* and shows the detail with which these professional lists are prepared.

CARING COMPLETELY
SHOT LIST

SCENE 1: JENNIFER'S LOUNGE

Establishing master two shot
Two shot Jennifer
Two shot Anne
Close up Jennifer
Close up Anne

SCENE 2: WALKING TO THE CLINIC

1. Pan/zoom with women to reveal porch with people waiting on it

SCENE 3: CLINIC WAITING AREA

1. MS Catherine pan to reveal women (greetings)
2. Two shot women dialogue about services and health ed. talk
3. Two shot women final dialogue as they move past waiting area
4. Reverse dialogue about health ed. talk (we see Sister Opus)
5. WS Sister Opus health ed. talk (through women in foreground)
6. MS Sister Opus health ed. talk (clean)
7. Reverse Sister Opus health ed. talk (women in background move)
8. Pan with women passing the waiting area and enter clinic

SCENE 4: INSIDE CLINIC

1. Wide establishing shot of women and deliver first lines through Jennifer leaving
2. MS Anne skeptical before sitting down
3. WS Jennifer introduces Anne
4. Two shot Jennifer sitting through scene
5. Two shot Okot sitting through scene
6. CU Jennifer sitting through scene
7. CU Okot sitting through scene
8. MCU Anne reaction throughout scene
9. MS to CU Zoom Anne thinking

SCENE 5

1. CU card, tilt, rack focus to MCU Muwanga (full scene)
2. Two shot Muwanga full scene

3. Two shot Jennifer full scene
4. CU Jennifer full scene
5. MCU cutaway speculum
6. WS establishing Anne observing (first half of scene)
7. MCU Anne reaction shot throughout scene

These shot lists are the guides on which crew members rely every day. When they arrive on location, all crew members must know exactly what to do in preparation for the first shot, and they must know exactly where to move equipment when the first shot is over.

SHOOTING SCHEDULES

The shooting schedule can be established once the locations have been identified and visited by key personnel (director, camera crew, sound crew), the actors have been selected and the scene visualization has been completed. Generally, for normal scenes, it is typical to shoot, at a minimum, 3–5 pages (or minutes) of the drama per shooting day. This means that one 30-minute video should be completed in 8–10 days, depending on the experience of the team and the complexity of locations, action and lighting requirements. Highly complex scenes, such as a traditional wedding, for instance, require considerably more time to set up and shoot than a simple conversation. The actual shooting schedule should be designed to make the most efficient use of time and actor availability.

CALL SHEETS

Call sheets are created to provide essential production information to everyone in the cast and crew on a daily basis. The information in a call sheet can include:

- The scenes scheduled for that day
- The location(s) where the day's filming will take place
- The actors required on that day
- Logistical information about transport arrangements for all required cast and crew to ensure that they reach the set on time
- Special requirements list: props, wardrobe, make-up
- Weather report, together with time of sunrise and sunset
- Catering arrangements (breakfast, lunch to be provided, etc.)
- Stand-by sequences, in case shooting gets ahead of schedule

Call sheets for the next day are typically prepared at midday every day based on what has been achieved in the morning and what is expected to be achieved during the afternoon. Call sheets are printed and given to all cast and crew members at the end of each day. An example of a call sheet appears here.

CALL SHEET #5
CHILDREN UNDER STRESS

Director	Taitsi	Producers:	Johnny
First A.D.	Garkayi		John
Line Producer:	Louise		Ben

Date: Friday, October 27

		Time	Crew	Cast	Extras
UNIT CALL	5:00 A.M.	**Breakfast** 6:00 A.M.	45	9	20
On Location	6:00 A.M.	**Lunch** 1:00 P.M.	45	9	20
Expected Wrap	5:00 P.M.				

Location: Clinic Well, Bush Road

Character	Artist	Pick up from–to	On Set
1. Tamari	Norman Mlambo	5:10 A.M. Home to Set	6:00 A.M.
4. Norah	Victoria Vuqeysha	5:10 A.M. Home to Set	6:00 A.M.
9. Ketiwe	Pelagia Viagi	4:25 A.M. Home to MFD	6:00 A.M.
14. Mr Zonde	Fidelis Chieza	4:00 A.M. Home to MFD	6:00 A.M.
18. Woman-well (1)	Chamaine Magwande	10:40 A.M. Home to MFD	12 noon
19. Woman-well (2)	Primrose Simbendi	10:00 A.M. Home to MFD	12 noon
20. Woman-well (3)	Tandi Matapasado	10:25 A.M. Home to MFD	12 noon
21. Nurse	Sizani Moyo	9:30 A.M. Antheneum Hall to set	10:30 A.M.
EX: Sick man	John Magwangi	4:00 A.M. Home to set	6:00 A.M.

SC. SET	ACTION	DAY/ NIGHT	CAST	PAGES
15. Clinic Ext.	Ketiwe, Tamari arrive clinic	D	1,4,9,14 + 16 extras	2/8
17. Clinic Ext.	Nurse tells Ket to go home	D	1,4,9,14 + 16 extras	1/8
16. Clinic Int.	Nurse examines Ket's card	D	1,21 EX + 16 extras	1/8
14. Bush Road	Zonde takes Ket to clinic	D	1,4,9,14 + 2 extras	6/8
85. Well	Woman rebukes Tamari	D	1,18,19,20 + 2 extras	1,3/8

ART DEPARTMENT: scotch cart; donkeys; whip; blanket for Ketiwe; clinic card; buckets; water on stand-by; firewood bundles; wheelchairs; stretchers; bags; etc., for extras in clinic.

EXTRAS Breakdown: 20—2 at well; 2 at Bush Road; 16 at clinic

ARRIVE PROMPTLY AT MFD AT 5:00 A.M.

Martin	Mara	Beulah	Jemma	
Temba	David	Rachel	Norah	Police

ARRIVE PROMPTLY AT SET AT 6:00 A.M.

Cornwell to leave set at 8:00 A.M. to go to MFD, then collect *Nurse* from Atheneum at 9:30 A.M. and bring to set. Then return to MFD to collect *women at well* from MFD. Isaac and Sekuru to collect later on: Phillip, Bernard, Nomsa, Pet, Lawrence. Then Isaac to collect *women at well 1,2,3,* from home to bring to MFD.

SPECIAL NOTES: *Drivers to confirm with Ashley and AD before they leave.*
No transport schedule for returning on Thursday. This will be circulated on Friday for Friday.

ADVANCE SCHEDULE: Monday October 30—Scenes 20,22,23,24.
ARTISTS REQUIRED: All rural
WEATHER: Cloudy periods with possible afternoon showers. Sunrise: 5:23 A.M. Sunset: 6:05 P.M.

Continuity Reports

Continuity reports are simple but vitally important forms that provide essential information on everything that is recorded on the camera (both picture and sound) during the shoot. A separate continuity report sheet or sheets (it might be necessary to allow several forms for each scene) should be prepared for each scene. Some scenes require more detailed information than others, but usually the information on the continuity report sheets needs to include the following points:

- The title of the drama
- The date of the shoot
- The number of each scene being covered
- The shot and take numbers
- The time code at the beginning of each shot
- A description of the shot: master shot; close-up of characters, etc.

- Comments on each shot: O.K. NG (no good); with—where necessary—an explanation for each NG recorded, such as "technical problems"; "creative problems"; "microphone visible."

The continuity reports are compiled by the Continuity Person whose job is to record all details completely and accurately. Sometimes the continuity person will make written notes to accompany the report if it is necessary to explain some items of the report in more detail. Continuity reports are a vital part of successful video and film creation. They ensure that each scene is completely covered with good "takes" of the various shots on the shot list. In Entertainment–Education dramas, it is sometimes necessary to mark "message problems" if the actor has failed to give the message details precisely or correctly in either speech or action. The shot might look and sound very good and the editor might be tempted to use it for artistic reasons, if it is not clearly marked "message problem (MP or Message!)" as identified by the Message Monitor.

Continuity reports also greatly assist the editing process because they allow the editor to identify quickly the best shots in the sequence, as well as any shots that should not be used. A sample Continuity Report appears here

---

SAMPLE CONTINUITY REPORT

Scene 33. Pg. 1   **DISH**
                                                                      Date: July 8

Time Code	Shot Description	Take #	Comment
	TAPE # 22		
22.08.24	close up Kato	1	NG
22.09.46	close up Kato	2	OK
22.11.31	2 shot Kato	1	OK
22.11.45	2 shot Kato	2	NG
22.11.03	2 shot Kato	3	Very good
22.13.50	2 shot Kato	4	NG
22.13.45	2 shot Kato	5	good
22.16.23	2 shot Catherine	1	good
22.18.16	2 shot Catherine	2	Message!
22.18.36	2 shot Catherine	3	good
22.20.26	2 shot Catherine	4	very good
22.22.14	wide shot, master	1	NG
22.22.32	wide shot, master	2	mic in shot
22.24.15	wide shot, master	3	good
22.26.07	close up Catherine	1	good
22.28.07	Mirembe reaction, mid	1	Very good
	CHANGE TAPE		

REVIEWING THE DAY'S WORK

It is essential to review each day's work before commencing the next day's work. The daily review can be done either at the end of the day or at the start of the following morning before shooting recommences, if the shoot is to be in the same place.

Reviewing confirms that pictures and sounds recorded during the day are acceptable. If the review reveals any problems—technical, creative or message related—arrangements must be made to pick up (repeat) these shots before the crew moves to the next location.

During the review, the information on the continuity forms can be checked against the time code to be sure it is correct. This confirmation process can be speeded up by checking only the "good" or "OK" takes on the continuity reports.

10

GUIDELINES FOR SUCCESSFUL SHOOTING

Photograph by John Riber

The drama should be filmed in such a way that it looks and sounds real.

FILM IS ILLUSION

All film, like all drama, is—in fact—illusion, not reality. In a good dramatic film, however, the viewers are drawn into the world of the characters and become emotionally involved with their circumstances, events, and feelings as if they were real. Even though they know they are watching a film, viewers easily become almost a part of the story. They laugh, cry, become angry, etc., just as the characters do. Viewers believe that the world they are watching is a REAL world. This is, of course, especially important in Entertainment–Education dramas, where it is the involvement with the characters and the story that has a lot to do with viewers' acceptance of the recommended behavior changes.

Maintaining the Illusion

It is very important that filmmakers maintain this illusion of reality. A good filmmaker ensures that nothing in the shooting of the film breaks the sense of reality for the audience. The drama must both look and sound real. Much of the achievement of this sense of reality has to do with technical detail. A believable film that looks and sounds good is not only about good acting and lighting, lenses and microphones; it is about **continuity** in dress, make-up, and location. It is also about such seemingly simple matters as matching the time of day and the weather in each sequence. A believable film cannot have, for example, one shot in a sequence where it is raining, and the rest of the shots in the same sequence when the sun is shining throughout, unless this is deliberately required by the script and commented on in the dialogue. Similarly, believability disappears if the characters suddenly change their clothes in mid-scene, or undergo a complete hair restyling between one mouthful of breakfast and the next.

CONTINUITY

Maintaining accurate continuity in all aspects of the film is one of the greatest challenges of good production. Film and video drama scenes are not shot in the order in which the script presents them or the audience sees them. The sequence of shooting is determined by other factors, such as location and actor availability. In determining the sequence of shooting, the director must take into account such questions as:

- When is a particular location available?
- How far away is the location?
- How many actors will have to be taken there?
- When will each of the actors be available?

Many actors, especially in developing countries, have other full-time jobs and it is often quite a challenge to create a shooting schedule that can accommodate the work schedules of all of them. The typical shooting arrangement, therefore, is that all sequences occurring in the same location are shot at the same time, before moving on to a new location. It is possible, therefore, that the very last scene of the drama could be shot first. The shooting sequence could begin with scenes from episode 26, followed by, for example, scenes from episodes 6 and 14. It is similarly possible that even scenes on the same location will be shot out of sequence, dependent upon actor availability and other factors. This is where the **continuity record** becomes so important. The following guidelines are helpful in maintaining control of all areas of continuity.

Continuity Guidelines

Pay Attention to Details of Costume

The term "costume" covers all aspects of the way a character looks in a scene: clothes, hairstyle, make-up, and overall personal presentation. If the character is looking somewhat sad in one sequence of the scene, it is important that this same feeling is presented in later sequences of this scene—unless something happens in the story to bring about a change in the character's demeanor. Even small details of clothing, such as beads or bangles, must be identical from one sequence of a scene to another. Similarly, if any characters have been involved in a fight or an accident that resulted in visible bruises, those bruises must be evident in the subsequent scenes and must slowly and naturally subside with the passage of time in the story. The audience may not be able to say exactly why the scene seems "uneven," but the smallest changes in clothing, hairstyle or make-up can give the audience a subconscious jolt and leave them with the feeling that something about the drama is not real.

Ensure Adequate Scene Coverage

The director must be sure that there is sufficient footage shot on the set for each sequence to allow the film editor to have options in putting the final picture together. A variety of shots allows the editor to avoid jump cuts* or clumsy continuity problems.

The following example shows the unreal feeling that a jump cut can generate in the audience:

> The camera is following a man, who is up to his waist in thick mud that is threatening to drag him down to his death. Suddenly the scene "jumps" to the same man sitting comfortably on the riverbank drinking a cup of tea.

The audience is left wondering: "How did that happen?" All sense of reality has disappeared because of the jump cut. In order to avoid jump cuts in the editing, the director must be sure that a variety of shots are taken. Every take of a sequence should be shot from various angles and in different frame sizes that give the editor a better chance of making the sequence seamless and believable. (See the section on "Shot Variety" below.)

Maintain the Position of Characters within the Frame

In a situation where two people are in conversation, the director should be sure that the characters remain on the same side of the screen in all shots, and are looking at each other in a consistent manner. One character will look consistently from left to right, and the other will look consistently from right to left. Once a character's line of vision is established, it must be carefully maintained in both direction and degree. If a character is looking at the other person with an eye-line of 20° at the outset of their conversation, then it must be maintained at 20°, unless there is a logical reason for it to change.

---

*Jump cuts are edits that break the continuity and consequently destroy the feeling of reality.

Maintain the Direction of Movement

If a character runs out of the scene, moving screen left to screen right, she must enter—in the next frame—from screen left and continue moving left to right. If it is necessary to change the direction to match a later shot in the sequence, then the character must turn and exit screen left and continue to move right to left.

Shot Variety

Frequently, only one camera will be used in shooting an Entertainment–Education drama, especially a low-budget drama. However, filming the same sequence from several different angles and editing the shots together can give the illusion that the scene has been covered by several cameras. Generally, each scene of a sequence that involves dialogue between two people should cover the dialogue in at least five different shots. These five shots can be achieved from three separate camera set-ups.

The Five Main Shots

The master shot
This is a wide shot that shows the location where the characters are. This long shot can be used throughout the entire scene. If the production can afford camera tracks, it can be very effective to open the scene with a wide shot and then track with the camera until it reaches a comfortable composition of the two characters speaking together.

Over-the-shoulder two shot
In this type of shot, the camera focuses on the face of one character (Character X) while showing the back or profile of the second character (Character Y). Characters should never look directly into the camera in drama, as reporters do in a newscast. In drama, the camera is observing the life of the characters, and allowing the audience the illusion of being an actual part of that life. When any character (even an "extra" walking through the scene) looks directly at the camera, the illusion is broken. It is as if the character is acknowledging the viewers as an audience, rather than including them as part of the fictional life.

The clean close-up shot
This shot can mostly be achieved from the same camera position as the over-the-shoulder two shot. Usually, it requires some lens adjustment to compose an in-focus close-up of, for example, Character X. It is also wise to adjust the camera position slightly for the "clean close-up" so that it is possible to go from an over-the-shoulder two shot to a "clean close-up" without risking a jump cut.

Reverse over-the-shoulder two shot
This is the same as the over-the-shoulder two shot, but in reverse, so that the camera is focusing on the face of Character Y, while showing the back or profile of Character X.

Reverse clean close-up
This is the same as the clean close-up shot, but taking in the other character: for example, Character Y.

Cut-aways
Whenever possible, it is a good idea to film cut-aways of each sequence. Cut-aways are shots that do not reveal any part of the face of the character who is speaking.

For example, a cut-away might show the hands of one of the characters, fiddling nervously with a button, or drumming a table in anger. Similarly, a cut-away could show a clock on the wall, reminding viewers that time is passing and, for example, the daughter of the family will soon return from school.

Cut-aways can be a real advantage during the editing of dialogue. If it is necessary to cut some words or sentences from a character's dialogue, the cut-away can be used to avoid jumping from one shot of the character's face directly to another facial shot. Similarly, cut-aways allow additional dialogue to be added without having to set up and shoot the whole scene again. The new lines can be recorded over ambient sound and edited in over the cut-away.

Confrontational and cooperative cross-cuts
Many directors like to follow a general rule that when the scene is confrontational (one character in direct conflict with another), the scene should be cross-cut, showing one character and then the other. When the scene is cooperative (the characters are in harmony with each other), the scene can be contained, with both characters in the same shot. In either case—even when the scene is cross-cut—the unbreakable rule is never to allow actors to look directly into each other's eyes. If they do look directly at each other, they destroy the audience's chances of seeing what each character is feeling. Actors who are supposed to be looking directly at each other should be placed on the set so that each is looking just to one side of the camera. In this way, each is visible to the audience, but their faces are also visible to the audience.

Scene Transition

As the drama moves from one scene (time or place) to another, it is important to make sure that one scene comes to a logical conclusion before moving to the next.
For example, a character who is sleeping soundly in bed at night should not appear in the next scene working in the office. There must be a logical link. In this case, the problem

could be overcome by showing the sleeping figure beginning to stir, yawn and sit up **as if about to rise for the day.** The office scene then fits in more logically as the audience can make a natural connection between waking up in the morning and going in to the office.

THE IMPORTANCE OF SOUND

Sometimes sound—especially background sound—might seem rather unimportant when compared with the overall film. Sound, however, is 50 per cent of film. It is easy to lose the audience's concentration and break the illusion of the story if the soundtrack lacks logical continuity.

Sound is too often overlooked during video productions, especially with low budget productions. The camera is treated like the star on the set and sound is often considered less important. Well-recorded, appropriate sound adds considerably to dramatic feeling.

Unfortunately, videotape is not the best format for recording location sound, and wherever possible—and affordable—location sound should be recorded separately on professional time-coded tape and later edited in to match the picture. This can be expensive and cumbersome, so where videotape is used, care must be taken to capture the best possible quality sound during the shoot. The selection and position of the microphones is of paramount importance. (It is not uncommon to see the camera operator and the sound recordist fighting for the best position on the set!) Well-recorded location sound will save a lot of time, effort and resources during the editing process. It should be remembered that sound deteriorates significantly with every generation (copy) that the videotape undergoes during editing.

During location shooting, the aim should be to have the dialogue as "clean" as possible. This means recording the dialogue **only** and no other simultaneous sound. Background (ambient) sound can be added during the editing session. So, while dialogue is being recorded, the director should ensure that

- any machines in the area are turned off.
- traffic is halted or re-routed.
- crowds are moved out of the way.
- anything that makes noise (such as a radio or a clock) is turned off.
- animals that are noisy or likely to make a noise are moved out of the way.

This will enable the recording of "clean" dialogue. During the editing, it is possible to choose and mix in other necessary sounds, such as cars passing, radio playing, telephones ringing, etc.

Some directors like to establish important or necessary background noises **in the** opening master shot. Then they turn off the noise for close-ups and any other shots where the source of the noise cannot be seen. If there is a need for shots where the "noise-maker" is seen while the characters are speaking, it can be recorded on wild dialogue tracks. Then, the clean dialogue is added during editing. It is wise also to record a long clean track of the ambient noise, so it can be mixed in at an appropriate level during editing without interrupting the dialogue.

Generally, the final step in professional high quality video post-production involves what is called "sound sweetening." This is usually done at a sound studio where the picture is locked to a digital or analog sound-recording system using time code. The location sound is then equalized and mixed with carefully recorded music and appropriate sound effects. Once the entire soundtrack is mixed and balanced on professional sound format, it is striped to the Master Picture Edit from which the broadcast and dubbing master tapes are made.

Music

All film or television drama requires at least some background music. Some directors like to have special theme music (even theme songs) created that will help to plant the story and the characters in the minds of the audience. When musicians are brought in to create special music, they should be advised of the nature of the project, the primary emotion the story wishes to arouse, and the audience(s) for whom the drama is designed. A copy of the design document is a useful tool for the musicians. If the music is really well-written and performed, it can be made available to the audience on CD. Some projects give CDs of the theme song or music as prizes for the quizzes that accompany the drama.

The Importance of Detail

It is surprising how even small details can affect the sense of reality of a visual presentation. The following list contains examples of detail errors that were overlooked in the finished edition of certain video productions:

- A young man leaving home with all his possessions in a suitcase is seen swinging the suitcase shoulder-high as he runs down the street. Obviously the prop suitcase was empty.
- A waiter carrying a tray loaded with teapots, kettles and cups into a restaurant puts down the tray and immediately picks it up again with one hand. Again, the props on the tray obviously were empty.

- A horse rolling in the sand is heard neighing. Horses cannot neigh while they are rolling on their backs. Farmers, for whom the film was made, had first-hand knowledge of horses.
- A man and woman are fighting over custody of a baby. They thrust the baby back and forth between them in a very active struggle. The baby makes no sound and her clothes and blanket stay intact throughout the whole scene. The baby is a doll. This would be a difficult scene to shoot with a real baby, but the use of the doll made the scene unbelievable and removed all sense of drama.
- A policeman looks at his watch and announces that it is ten o'clock. The clock on the wall behind him—which is in clear view—indicates that it is three o'clock. Nothing is ever said about the wall clock not working.

It is tempting to think that the audience will not notice small details like these, but they do, and this can make a difference to the believability of the scene. Even if viewers cannot identify the exact problem, they have a sense, nevertheless, that there is something wrong with the scene. The dedicated director ensures that no detail errors are left in the finished production, even if it means calling on outside experts (such as a horse farmer) to ensure accuracy.

STOCK FOOTAGE

Stock footage is film that has been shot in the past for some other film or video production and "borrowed" for the current production. The temptation often is to use stock footage for events that are difficult to arrange at short notice. Such events as a hurricane, an airplane crash, or a landslide cannot be ordered up by a film director just when they are needed. The difficulty with stock footage, however, is that it is often of inferior quality because it has been around for a long time or it has been copied so often that it is now down to the fourth or fifth generation. As a result, the stock footage looks unreal when edited into the modern film. Avoiding the need for stock footage really lies with the script-writer and with the script reviewers. They must ensure that the success of the picture does not rely on showing an event that is virtually impossible to film. Reference to the event can be made in the dialogue, and characters can be seen reacting to the aftermath of the event, but in the interests of reality, impossible-to-shoot scenes should be avoided.

SPECIAL EFFECTS

A well-written, well-enacted and well-directed Entertainment–Education drama does not need an overdose of audio and visual effects. The drama is "imitating life," not creating a highly imaginative space odyssey. Real life is not embroidered with blinding flashbacks, rapid zooms into the future, or echo effects added to the background of human voices. Sometimes a special effect, such as a dissolve, can overcome a really tricky editing problem. (Hence the saying, "if you can't solve it, dissolve it!") Generally, however, it is better to determine from the outset of the shoot what special sound or picture effects are really essential to the finished drama.

KNOWING THE SUBJECT MATTER

If the script calls for an event with which the director and crew members are unfamiliar (such as vaccinating infants), it is essential to find out all the details before the shoot begins. Speaking to an expert on the subject can be helpful, but more important is actually *seeing* an example of the event in advance of the shoot. It is not enough to have a verbal description of what should happen or is likely to happen in a particular situation. In order for the event to be shot effectively, it must be viewed by the director and the camera crew so they can determine the best possible shooting approach.

USING CHILDREN AND BABIES

It is wise to avoid, as much as possible, the use of young children and babies. Babies are very likely to become upset with all the noise and activity of a film shoot. They often cry or even scream just when the script calls for them to be happy. If it is essential to have a baby in the scene, it is helpful to show the baby in the master shot, and then shoot around it. The camera crew can shoot a few close-ups of the baby while he or she is peaceful so that these can be edited in later. Otherwise, it is best to avoid shooting the baby as much as possible, and edit in background noises of the baby as needed. If there must be a baby in the film, as, for example, in a film containing a message about infant nutrition, it helps to make sure that the mother is nearby all the time to soothe and quiet the baby as needed.

Young children can also be a problem in films. They tire and become bored when they have to repeat lines or actions over and over again. It is often difficult for them to learn their lines and speak them naturally. Children can be used in background and cut-away scenes, but it is usually best to avoid having very young children in starring roles.

Good shooting begins with adequate preparation and is enhanced by the close cooperation of the program manager, the director, the camera operators and the sound operators.

PART 5

For the Actors/Artists

11

GUIDELINES FOR
SUCCESSFUL ACTING

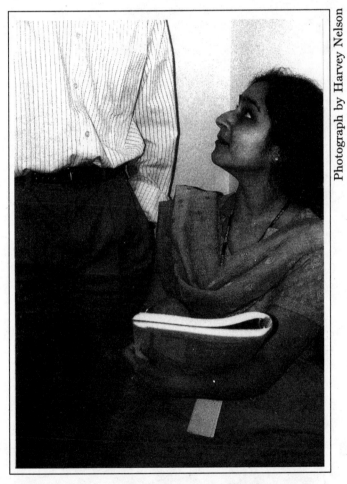

Photograph by Harvey Nelson

Actors must learn to fit movements within the camera
frame, so that important elements are not omitted.

CHARACTERISTICS OF FILM AND TELEVISION ACTING

Film directors generally believe that film should tell the major part of the story through pictures rather than through words. While this may be true for film, the rule must be interpreted slightly differently for television because television viewers are more easily distracted than film viewers.

There are few distractions in a movie theater; people are not in their own homes so they are not tempted to run to the refrigerator for a snack or dash off to answer the telephone in another room. A movie, therefore, can afford to have fairly long pictorial sequences with little or no dialogue because the audience is virtually forced to watch them. With television, the viewers' attention can be drawn away from the screen relatively easily. Usually there is some light on while the family watches television, so family members are able to see other activities in the room. Similarly, the kitchen, the bathroom, the telephone, the crying baby—these are all within reach and can distract the television audience easily. Once they look away from the screen, they tend to lose the point very quickly if the point relies on a visual image. Dialogue helps refocus attention and fill in gaps in a way that a visual image alone cannot. Moreover, the sound on the television set can be turned up to a surprisingly loud pitch if someone wants to hear the dialogue from another room.

Visual images are important in television, nevertheless, and must be given very careful consideration by the writer and the director. But it is equally important to ensure that the story is adequately covered by dialogue as well as by action. The way in which the actors deliver the dialogue is as important in television acting as it is in radio and on stage, but television and film actors have an added challenge. Like stage actors, they can be seen by the audience as well as be heard, so everything they do, every move they make, as well as every word they utter will have an effect on the overall success of the drama. Unlike stage actors, however, the television actor is often seen only partially (in close-up, for example), so he must use a certain amount of "cheating," such as exaggeratedly slow or overly dramatic movements, in order to make the picture look real.

GUIDELINES FOR ACTING

The following guidelines can assist actors and directors in ensuring that characters presented on the screen are believable:

Knowing the story

One of the major differences between stage or street-theater acting and film or video acting is that on stage or the street, the actors start at the beginning of the drama and act their way through to the end in the logical sequence of the story. In film and television shooting this progression is often not maintained. Because all the scenes in one location are shot at the same time, actors might be called upon to act out the major climax of the drama before they perform the developing conflicts, or to act out the finale before the first scene has been shot.

Box 11.1
10 GUIDELINES FOR ACTING
1. Knowing the story
2. Interpretation
3. Reaction
4. Gestures
5. Props
6. Framing
7. Voice moderation
8. Speaking speed
9. Volume
10. Acting for the lens

It may happen (perhaps at the end of the shooting day), that an actor might have to perform some scenes alone, when all other actors have left the set. In such cases, the actor has to react to words and actions that are not occurring in front of her or him. These situations can sometimes make it difficult for actors to evoke the appropriate emotions. Acting is much easier if actors and the director are familiar with the whole story. Actors should avoid the temptation to learn only their own lines and to know nothing of the rest of the story. A good Entertainment–Education director will take the time to sit down with all the actors, tell them the story, help them understand the message that the story wishes to convey, and advise them on the emotional focus the story will emphasize in order to motivate appropriate behavior change. When a scene is being shot out of sequence, the director should remind the actors of the scene's place in the story, the relationship of the scene to the hoped for behavior change in the audience, and the emotion that should be stressed.

Interpretation

The actor's job is to bring the story to life for the viewers. In Entertainment–Education drama, actors have the added responsibility of blending the message into the story believably. They must avoid changing from being actors to being lecturers every time some aspect of the message is included in the story. Part of this message blending is the responsibility of the writer; part of it depends on the character interpretation developed by the actors and the director. Actors should feel completely comfortable "in the skin" of the characters they are asked to portray. When an actor is called upon to portray a personality type with which he is not familiar, he should make it his business to find and observe such people carefully and learn how to present them believably.

Reaction

Every television actor must learn to *react* to what is being said by another actor or other actors in the scene, and to the action taking place in the scene. While these reactions must look natural, most of them are to some degree exaggerated. In normal conversation, it is not unusual for two people to talk together for quite some time without any visible reaction on either face. If two people do this on television, they will look "dead" and bored and inspire the same reactions in their audience. It must be remembered that drama never, in fact, records "normal" conversation. There is always a point to what the characters are saying—a point that contributes to the action and conflict of the plot. Similarly, the reactions of the actors help the audience understand both the conflict and the emotion of the story. Actors should be encouraged to react to the speaker's words *before the speaker has finished speaking and before saying their own lines*. In the same way, those who are speaking should include any important actions or reactions before finishing their lines, not after. Good editing usually cuts from the speaker to the listener's reactions before the speaker's words are finished. Consequently any actions performed after the final words would be lost.

In Entertainment–Education drama, the actors' reactions can be beneficial in motivating audience behavior.

For example: Consider how facial reaction would affect the audience in the following scene:

1. MOTHER My dear husband, the schoolteacher came by today. He told me that our daughter could start school next month.
2. FATHER Our daughter is going to school? What are you saying?
3. MOTHER The teacher said she could. What do *you* think?
4. FATHER Well ... I think ... I think ... it's amazing....

Clearly, this scene could be interpreted in a number of ways. In the split second after the mother's words, the audience will have their own subconscious reaction to what she has said. Those who are in favor of education for girls of all ages will want the father to be pleased, but will be afraid that he might not agree (conflict). Those who disapprove of girlchild education will hope the father will be angry, but they might have some fear that he will like the idea (conflict again). It is the *immediate facial reaction* of the father—even before he says a word—that advises the audience of the direction of the plot, and, subtly, of the message.

In shooting this scene, the shot list might be as follows:

1. Master shot (wide) of father coming into the house as mother is preparing tea.
2. Medium shot of mother as she turns to husband and speaks. (The expression on mother's face as she delivers these lines is not seen in close-up. Her face and body movement, however, are important and will be determined by such things as the relationship between the husband and wife, the message, where the line comes in the plot, and whether or not suspense is needed at this point.)
3. Close-up of father's face showing reaction to the wife's remarks.
4. Close-up of father speaking, OR
5. Two shot of father and mother showing mother's bodily reaction to father's words (e.g., backing away from him in fear, or going towards him in happiness).

Shot 3 is a defining moment in the story, and in the message. The audience sees the father's facial reaction—briefly—before he speaks. If the father's face is scowling, the audience is aware immediately that he is against the idea. If the father has a questioning expression on his face, the audience will know he is not sure about the idea, as indeed some audience members might be similarly unsure. If the father is smiling broadly, the audience knows he feels good about the school idea and perhaps some of them subconsciously wonder if they should feel the same way. With radio, the audience would have to rely on the father's **vocal interpretation** of the words to understand his feelings. With stage performances, the audience would see and hear the reaction at the same time. With video, it is vital that the response is observed first in the visual reaction and then in the words.

The truth is that when there are two speakers on the screen in a drama, the audience is more inclined to watch the listener than the speaker. This is because they are interested in knowing what effect the speaker will have on the listener. This fact about drama watchers further reinforces the importance of actors learning to *react* to words and situations. Actors should be given exercises in reacting to various situations.

Gestures

Reactions can be expressed on the actor's face or through his/her gestures. Hand gestures can be very expressive of a person's inner feelings. A clenched fist can indicate anger, fear, or pain. Hands clasped together can suggest nervousness or anxiety. The tapping hand represents impatience while hands raised with fingers outspread can suggest surprise. Feelings can be expressed also with shoulder movements. Shoulders can be raised in exasperation, slumped in despair, or raised and lowered swiftly as a sign of indifference or ignorance. Actors should practice showing reactions through body movements as well as through facial expression so that their feelings can be understood even when they are not shot in close-up. It is helpful for actors to study real human beings to determine what types of gestures are common to certain personalities. Many gestures tend to be culture-specific, so that gestures typical in one society might be quite unknown to another. Actors who are playing roles in serial drama should develop culturally appropriate gestures characteristic of their screen persona—gestures by which the audience will recognize the character and the character's personality.

For example, an egotistical person might have the habit of stamping his foot every time he starts to speak, just to be sure of attracting attention. A kind, loving person might have the habit of putting her hand over her heart every time she feels moved or concerned about other people. Gestures, carefully and correctly used, can do a lot to enhance an actor's performance and guide the audience's feelings towards the characters and towards the desired behavior change.

Props

"Props," as mentioned earlier, is the short form of the word "properties". Television actors should learn to make appropriate use of props as another means of showing feeling. The appropriate use of props also provides effective cut-away opportunities that can be really helpful during editing. The thoughtful, experienced actor never remains completely motionless and expressionless (unless in a state of complete shock) while another actor or other actors are speaking. There are some directors who claim that actors should never be completely still; they should always be engaged in some type of action or reaction, however minimal.

The following description of the actions and reactions of secondary actors in a scene shows the value of using props appropriately.

Scene: A Restaurant

A group of teenagers is enjoying some drinks and snacks. One of the boys, Jack, starts to flirt with one of the girls, Susan. Jack's actions are as follows: he moves closer to Susan; he puts his hand on hers; he runs his hand slowly up her arm; he moves his face closer to hers; he whispers in her ear.

The other two teenagers can see what is going on. Their actions and reactions indicate how they feel about the situation. The girl, Meg, is embarrassed. She puts her hand over her mouth as she giggles; she pretends to drop her purse on the floor so she can bend down and avoid having to watch. The boy, Mike, is angry and jealous. He flips through the menu, trying to call Jack's attention to items on it by pointing at them with his straw; he blows bubbles in his drink through his straw; he tries to balance the straw on the edge of the glass. Finally, he blows a straw full of juice directly at Jack.

Framing

The field of vision in television is relatively small and confined within the "frame" of the picture the viewers can see. This means that any action or reaction, or any important prop must be within that relatively small frame if it is to be seen by the audience. Consequently, actors and directors must learn to think within the frame and ensure that everything they want the audience to see is within that frame. This need often requires that characters be much closer together than they would be in real life or on the stage. Many actors, and indeed many inexperienced directors, make the mistake of placing characters in a scene in "natural" positions. For example, they place two people who are having a conversation on opposite sides of the room. This leads to what can be called "ping-pong" shooting where the shot cuts backwards and forwards (like the ball in a ping-pong or table tennis game) from one face to the other depending upon who is speaking or whose reactions are being filmed. When characters are far apart like this, it becomes virtually impossible to do a two shot, or even a reverse shot where the camera is looking at the speaker over the shoulder of the listener. If two people in a conversation must be placed apart (for reasons of the story), then they should be placed in the room in such a way that with a long shot or even a medium shot it is possible to have both in the frame. It is also very helpful to place them so that the camera can go behind one or other of the characters to take an over-the-shoulder shot.

When a character has a hand action, such as drumming the fingers in irritation, the actor must ensure that the action takes place within the frame. Perhaps, instead of drumming the fingers on the arm of the chair (as might be normal), the actor could drum her fingers on her own shoulder or collarbone so that the action is within the frame. Acting for TV means constantly thinking about the screen size and the picture frame as well as about conveying emotions. Many actions that are associated with traditional crafts such as sewing, knitting, painting and pottery-making might require "cheating" if there is a need for a close-up of the artist's face while he works. The artist's table might have to be raised higher than normal; the piece of embroidery might have to be brought much closer to the sewer's face than is normal, etc. Television acting, more than stage acting, does require the actor to be willing and able to adopt unusual (sometimes uncomfortable) positions and poses to accommodate the picture frame.

Voice moderation

Many inexperienced actors believe that if they learn and deliver their words accurately, they will be doing a good job. Too often, the result of such an approach is a torrent of words that lack real feeling and are often misinterpreted or not understood by the audience.

Actors should be encouraged to watch real people speaking and to note how often people stop mid-sentence to think or just to catch their breath, repeat themselves, scratch their heads or tap their fingers, etc. A good actor imitates this realism to some extent. An exact copy of real people in a conversation could be irritating to the viewers because there would be too many hesitations and sidetracks. The actor must learn to **moderate** between real speech and acted speech. It is helpful for actors to think about how they want their viewers to feel as a result of what they are saying and to stress—in some way—those words that are likely to evoke the appropriate feeling. Interpretation means not only the tone of voice, but also the speed of delivery, the positioning of pauses and the stress on chosen words.

For example, the following lines could have several meanings depending on how the actor delivers each line and on what he wants the audience to feel. The underlining indicates the words that the actors should stress in the delivery and the slanted marks// indicate where the actor must pause very briefly. Notice that the speed of delivery is affected by stresses and pauses.

(Feeling: horror)

<u>This</u> is an <u>amazing</u> day.// I <u>honestly</u> did not believe <u>I</u> would be alive to see a day// like this. // When I <u>consider</u> what the <u>leaders</u> of this country have <u>done</u>,// I cannot help but wonder// what the <u>future</u> will bring.// <u>Why</u> are <u>these</u> things// happening in <u>our</u> country?// What <u>will</u> happen next?

(Feeling: joy)

<u>This</u> is an <u>amazing</u> day.// I <u>honestly</u> did not believe I would be alive to see <u>a day like this</u>. // When I consider what the <u>leaders of this country</u> have done, I cannot help but <u>wonder</u> what the future will bring.// Why are these things happening in <u>our</u> country? What <u>will</u> happen next?

Speaking speed and action speed

An interesting characteristic of human beings is that they tend to adjust their speech to the speed of their physical movement. A person rushing to get ready to leave home in the morning might tumble out clipped words and sentences at a great pace. A person sitting happily and lazily by a swimming pool in the sun is more likely to have a slow speech pattern with leisurely breaks between words and sentences. Acting for television requires an adjustment of this normal behavior. Actors must learn to slow down their movements so that the camera can follow what they are doing. At the same time, their words must not be slowed down but must be delivered at a normal pace. A simple movement such as taking a thermometer from a patient's mouth and reading the temperature must be slowed down deliberately if the camera is meant to be following the action. If filmed at its normal speed, this action would look jerky and disruptive or it would not be observed at all. If the actor is speaking while using and reading the thermometer, she must be careful that she does not slow down her speech to match her movements.

Even getting up out of a chair might require a change in normal movement if the camera is trying to stay on the actor's face. Frequently, people getting up from an armchair will lower their heads as they press their hands down on the chair's arms and push their bodies up. Such an action takes the face out of the camera range. The actor must learn to stand up without lowering the face, and, if speaking at the same time, be sure that while movements are somewhat artificial and slower than usual, speech is at a completely normal speed.

Volume

Another characteristic of the human voice is that as people speak faster; their voices tend to get louder. Television actors have to learn to contradict this tendency deliberately. Even as the speed and energy of the voice is maintained, the volume must be kept moderate. Actors who are experienced in stage or street theater sometimes have trouble adjusting to video acting because they are accustomed to projecting their voices to reach the outer edges of the crowd. With television and film, the rule is to project only as far as the microphone. This does not mean that actors should look at the microphone, but it does mean they should be aware of where the microphone is and try to ensure that their voices will reach the microphone comfortably. Actors should learn to pay close attention when the sound recorder takes the voice levels. This action is not just to help the recorder be sure he has the volume up loud enough and that there are no extraneous noises interrupting; it also lets the actors know how far and how loudly they should project their voices.

Acting for the lens

Just as actors must adjust their voice volume to reach no further than the microphone, so they should bear in mind that their audience is the camera lens. This means ensuring that every action and reaction fits comfortably and naturally (even if it is uncomfortable and unnatural during the acting) into the space allowed by the camera lens. But, acting for the camera lens does not mean looking at the camera lens. An actor in a drama should *never* look directly at the lens. It means being aware of the small size of the picture and the limitations of space within which the actions and reactions must be shown.

Acting alone

Some actors feel very uncomfortable if they have to perform a scene with no other actors present. Others, professionals as well as beginners, actually prefer to deliver their lines (particularly lines that are especially dramatic or powerful) without other actors present. It seems that they can "get into the role" better when no other actor is watching them. Directors should be aware of this and allow actors with long or important speeches to try it both ways (with and without other actors present) and see which works better.

USING "LOCALS" AS ACTORS

When making Entertainment–Education dramas on a limited budget, some directors choose to use, in minor roles, local people with no previous acting training or experience. This practice certainly saves money, but it can have a detrimental effect on the quality of the film (and therefore perhaps on its effectiveness) if the untrained actors are also unconvincing. The following brief guidelines can help make untrained actors more convincing.

Guidelines for Untrained Actors

Stress emotion

Encourage the actors to think how *they* would feel if the events of the story happened to them in real life. Sometimes it helps to re-tell the story using the names of appropriate members of the actors' families so they can gain a more realistic sense of what these events would do to their feelings if they happened in their lives.

Use the actor's words

Let untrained actors try expressing the lines in their own words, rather than in the scripted words. Read the exact words to the actor, then explain the emotional meaning of the lines and then let the actor try a personal interpretation of the words. As long as the message is not compromised and the real feeling and meaning of the words are the same as the original intention, this approach can work.

Record more than is needed

Untrained actors tend to feel very pressured if they are required to wait for the director to signal "Action" and then recite their lines. It is sometimes better to get the sound and the camera rolling casually and then invite the actor to "go through the lines once or twice." It is not uncommon for untrained actors to give a much better performance in a casual run through like this than in a prepared performance.

Provide reaction

It is also often easier for untrained actors to maintain the required emotional and physical interpretation of their lines if there is someone reacting to what they do and say. It can be helpful to "plant" someone on the set (but off camera) who can respond naturally and encouragingly to the actors as they deliver the lines. At the same time, it should be re-membered that many non-actors become easily embarrassed if there is a crowd watching their performance. It is generally better to keep the shooting area free of spectators while shooting is taking place.

Limit shooting time

Acting can be a strenuous mental activity even for trained and experienced actors. For inexperienced actors, being in front of the camera for any length of time can be almost traumatic. Recording short takes of no more than two to three minutes at a time can assist untrained actors to give acceptable performances. If this is done, it is important to take a sufficient number of cut-away shots so that editing does not become a problem.

Provide a sightline

The natural tendency for all inexperienced actors is to look directly into the lens of the camera. Even when amateurs start out looking where the director has asked them to look, it is difficult for them to keep their eyes from wandering back to the lens. This problem can be overcome by asking them to look at a particular person who is standing in the correct sight line. This person can be instructed to wave briefly if he sees the actor's eyes shifting in the wrong direction. The movement of the briefly waving hand is usually enough to bring the actor's wandering eyes back to the right place.

Use patience and encouragement

Citizens and community members who are being used as extras (actors other than the main characters) in a social development drama should be encouraged to think that there is plenty of time for them to become comfortable in their roles. Even when time is limited and everything is under time pressure, the director should try not to let this become apparent to the extras. Pressure creates pressure and inexperienced actors who feel they are being pressured or criticized are far more likely to make repeated mistakes than those who feel a sense of calm and encouragement around them at all times.

In an Entertainment–Education project, all actors, whether professional or amateur, should be encouraged to appreciate the value of what they are doing for the people who will view the drama. Their presentation of the drama and its messages can change lives and even save lives. Actors and production crew members should be reminded of this from time to time and thanked for the valuable contribution they are making to the betterment of society.

PART 6

For the Evaluators

12

PILOT TESTING

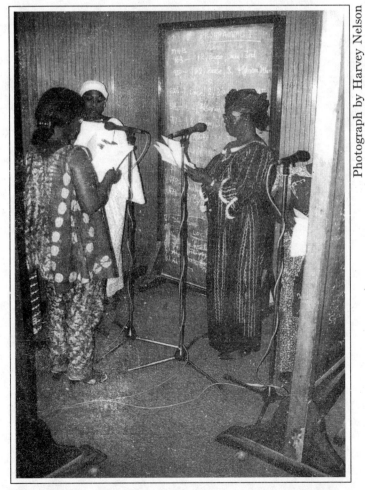

Photograph by Harvey Nelson

Film and video dramas can be pilot tested with audio recording to save time and money.

THE IMPORTANCE OF THE PILOT TEST

Before going ahead with the final scripting and production of a television serial drama, it is vital to pilot test the story with members of the intended audience(s). The pilot test is the measure of whether the audience will

- be attracted to the story and want to find out what is going to happen.
- be attracted to the characters and recognize them as people with whom they can relate.
- understand the message(s) and recognize the relevance of these messages to their lives.

Some program managers and directors like to test the synopsis with members of the audience before even beginning the scriptwriting process. Synopsis testing is certainly wise when the audience is unaccustomed to watching film or television. Synopsis testing also helps determine if the overall story and the characters are attractive to the audience and likely to hold their attention.

Whether or not synopsis testing is done, pilot testing of three episodes should be done with several groups of representative audience members. It can be carried out in focus group discussions, or through written evaluations, or both. When using focus groups, it might be necessary to have separate groups for men and for women, or for adults and adolescents if it seems likely that one group could influence the other during the discussion.

The main areas for which the test seeks information from the audience are:

1. **Accepting the drama:** The audience accepts the drama, the characters, and the messages as relevant to their lives.
2. **Understanding the drama:** The audience understands the plot, the setting, the action, and the characters of the drama because these components are relevant to their own lives.

3. **Trusting the drama messages:** The audience trusts the messages in the drama because they are presented in a relevant manner by people (characters) in whom the audience would willingly place their trust in real life.
4. **Finding the drama attractive:** The drama has sufficient and appropriate *emotional* attraction to hold the attention of the chosen audience(s). They are eager to know what is going to happen in the story.
5. **Appreciating the drama:** They are interested in the story, the characters, and the messages and are ready and willing to watch the drama on a regular basis.

Focus Group Sample Questionnaire

The following Focus Group Discussion Questions and Individual Self-Administered Questionnaire can be used as guidelines for reviewing Entertainment–Education television dramas. These questions can be discussed in the order given, or the focus group leader might prefer to give questions about the drama ahead of questions about the message.

FOCUS GROUP DISCUSSION GUIDE

Topic	Suggested Questions
Recognition	1. What information in the drama do you think might be useful for the health and safety of the audience?
	2. How useful is this information to most viewers?
	3. Which information was new to you? What did you learn about for the first time?
	4. What are the main attributes or qualities of each of the main characters? What are they like?
Comprehension	1. In your words, what is the story really about?
	2. What part of the story is difficult to understand?
	3. What part of the story might you want to change? How?
Persuasiveness	1. Do you think that the information in the story will persuade/convince your friends to change some of their current practices? Why/why not?
	2. Do you have any suggestions to increase the persuasiveness of the story and the messages?

(Contd)

(*Contd*)

Acceptability and Appropriateness

1. Are the messages/story acceptable in your local community?
2. Is there any message that may be offensive or unacceptable to the real situation/customs in your community? What message? Why? In what way are they unacceptable?
3. About whom do you think the story is talking? People like you or other people? (What other people?)
4. How much do you care about what happens to the main characters in the story? Which one do you care about the most? Why?

Credibility

1. Do you think that the story is believable? Could it happen in real life? Why/why not?

Level of Enjoyment

1. How much did you like this drama compared to others that you have seen on television recently? What did you like the most? Why?
2. What did you dislike about the story? Why?
3. While listening, did you, at any point, begin to lose interest in the story? When? Why?
4. What changes do you think would most improve the story?
5. What do you feel after hearing the story?

INDIVIDUAL SELF-ADMINISTERED QUESTIONNAIRE
PRETEST OF SERIAL DRAMA SCRIPTS

We are seeking your reactions to the serial drama episodes. We believe that you are the best person to make comments on our scripts. Your contribution is invaluable in helping us make the serial drama successful. Information collected from this questionnaire will be kept confidential and used only for revising the scripts.

By answering all questions, you are contributing to improving health for people in our nation.

Province: .... District: ....

Ward/Commune: .... Date: ..../........../...................

Identification of respondents

Line No.	Questions	Answers	Code
1.	[Please indicate whether the respondent is male or female]	Male Female	1 2
2.	How old are you?	Age	–
3.	What is your ethnic group?	Major ethnic group Other/specify	1 2
4.	What is your highest level of education?	Primary (1–5) Secondary (6–9) High School (10–12) Vocational school/College University None Other/specify	1 2 3 4 5 6 7
5.	What is the **major job** you do monthly to make money?	Agriculture Forestry Business Government cadre Retired Student/pupil Housewife Casual labourer Unemployed Other/specify	1 2 3 4 5 6 7 8 9 10
6.	What is your current marital status?	Married Single Separated Divorced Widow Defacto	1 2 3 4 5 6

In the space provided, please write down your answers, giving as much detail as possible.

7. What is the story about?
8. If your friends ask you "what do you learn from the drama?", what do you tell them?
9. Please list some health messages that are most important in the drama?
10. What characters do you like most? Why?
11. Could you please write down something about each character you mentioned?
12. What characters do you like least? Why?
13. Please write down something about each character you mentioned.
14. What do you like most in the drama? Why?
15. What do you like least in the drama? Why?
16. What information in the drama is new to you?
17. For whom do you think this drama is designed?
18. What would you recommend to make the drama more useful?

Before ending, please double-check all questions to ensure that all of them are answered.

METHODS OF PILOT TESTING TELEVISION DRAMAS

Pilot testing television drama presents a challenge. To actually film and edit three episodes of a TV drama series is both expensive and time consuming. Usually, it is possible to do an effective pilot test of a TV drama series without actually filming it.

Pilot testing can be done by:

1. having artists read and act out the script(s) in front of the focus group.
2. using a storyboard to show the audience what the visuals would look like, while having artists read the script.
3. doing a very quick and rough shoot of one or two scenes (unedited) of an episode. As well as having actors reading the full script of one or two episodes, this rough shoot can be shown to the audience to give them a sense of what the finished visuals will be like.
4. preparing an audio recording of the video script and using that for the pilot testing.

Pilot Testing with an Audio Recording

The use of an audio recording of the script is often the most successful way of pilot-testing the drama. Audio recording is far less costly than filming, and allows for the recording and testing of three episodes relatively inexpensively. The audio recording certainly makes it possible to judge the five pilot test areas listed on pages 221–22. There are some guidelines that should be followed in preparing the audio pilot test. The obvious difference between TV and radio is that the audience cannot see what is happening on radio. For this reason, the pilot script must be adapted so that the audience can understand all the action even when they cannot see it.

Guidelines for Pilot Testing a TV Drama with an Audio Recording

1. Characters should address each other by name, especially at the beginning of a scene, so that the listeners know who is in the scene.
2. An Announcer or Narrator should be used at the beginning of the episode to remind the audience of what has happened in the story so far or to introduce the story in Episode 1.
3. Important action must be described (naturally) because it cannot be seen. For example, if a character sees a friend riding a motorcycle along the road, he should make a comment, such as "Chaka always rides that motorbike far too fast."
4. Sound effects (SFX) should be used when necessary to indicate location: e.g., traffic in the background when characters are in the street.
5. Scenes should be connected through dialogue when possible. At the end of one scene, a character talks about something that is going to happen in the next scene, and this allows a natural transition from one scene to the other without using music (see lines 27 and 29 of sample script on page 229).
6. Use music briefly to separate one scene from the next.
7. Indicate to the actors that they should move (without changing their voice level) towards the microphone to suggest that they are coming into the scene and away from the microphone when they are going out. These moves are indicated in brackets in capital letters within the character's speech, e.g.:

MAJID	(COMING IN) Where is everybody?
JODA	(GOING OUT) They're all on their way to the fair. Come on!

8. Use the announcer or narrator at the end of the episode to raise questions, remind the audience of the message in a subtle way, and invite the audience to listen to the next episode.

9. Set out the script in the manner in which this example is set out. Number the dialogues (speeches). **Never** allow a dialogue in an audio script to be divided between one page and the next. A dialogue divided between two pages is harder for the radio actor, who is reading from the script while recording, to read effectively.

10. Select actors who have voices suited to the age of the character and who have voices distinctly different from each other. If possible, use the same artists who will be portraying the characters in the video performance.

Sample Audio Pilot Test Script

The following is a sample of an audio version of an episode from the Vietnam TV drama serial, *"Overcoming Challenge"*, the full TV script of which is given in Chapter 4.

OVERCOMING CHALLENGE
Pilot Test—Audio Episode # 1   Page 1 of 7

---

1. MUSIC. THEME MUSIC UP: 10 secs. FADE UNDER NARRATION

2. NARRATOR   Today we begin a story that everyone will enjoy. It is a love story, a mystery story, a comedy—something for everyone. As our story begins we meet a young man, Quang, walking by West Lake Water Park in Hanoi with his girlfriend, Ngan. Let's join them as they walk.

3. MUSIC UP BRIEFLY AND FADE UNDER SFX.

4. SFX. CROWD NOISES ... HOLD BRIEFLY AND FADE UNDER DIALOGUE AND OUT

5. QUANG   (MID SENTENCE) In fact, there is nothing new when writing about drug abuse but it is never outdated. Closely relating to this problem is fate ....

6. NGAN   But Quang, to tell the truth ... being in charge of a research is different from being just a member of the research team! I'm very worried as you have just been working for the Youth Research Institute for more than a year and you are not experienced.

7. QUANG   Experience cannot just come by itself.... We gain experience from doing.

OVERCOMING CHALLENGE
Pilot Test—Audio Episode # 1

8. NGAN

(GIGGLING) You sound very confident! Do you feel uncomfortable in front of those with MA and Doctorate degrees at the Institute?

9. QUANG

Why do I have to feel uncomfortable? They have also undergone the period I'm in now. If I don't know, I will ask…. But I feel self-confident as you said. Without this characteristic, it is very difficult to fulfil our work.

10. NGAN

(THOUGHTFULLY) Your project is called "Current situation of drug abuse and utilisation of addictive substances among the youth"…. How useful are the results of the research?

11. QUANG

(TEASINGLY) You claim yourself a newspaper reporter of social investigation and yet you ask "What use are the results?" They are very useful for youth organisations in preventing the spread of drug addiction…. You will also need my research as it will provide information for your long newspaper story. OK?

12. NGAN

(LOVINGLY) I need you or you need me? It is I who will advertise your research free of charge…. Don't take advantage of my *Thanh Xuan* newspaper. Remember!

13. QUANG

It is foolish of me not to take advantage of the newspaper, it is ours! Of course, I will have to go to the field soon to collect data. I don't want the results of my research to be simply a meaningless report.

14. NGAN

But how do you plan to do it? Where do you plan to do it?

15. QUANG

(LAUGHING) What makes you panic, Ngan?

16. NGAN

I know you very well. It is reasonable to be worried, isn't it? Please tell me, what is your plan?

17. QUANG

(SOMEWHAT CONFUSED) I … I will go to some dens of the drug addicts, for example….

18. NGAN

That's why I'm scared! They are dangerous places. Why don't you try other measures?

OVERCOMING CHALLENGE
Pilot Test—Audio Episode #1   Page 3 of 7

19. QUANG	Like what?
20. NGAN	(RESOLUTELY) Don't try to challenge me.... But until I think of another way, you have to promise to me that you are not going to do anything without discussing with me. Is it OK?
21. QUANG	I promise.... How tough you are. After our marriage, perhaps I have to submit to you my plan of action day after day, haven't I?
22. NGAN	It's not bad! I won't have to worry, as long as you are not pushy.
23. QUANG	Give me your hand. You know I love you. We will organise our wedding party at the end of the year.
24. NGAN	No.... This year is not my year. Let's make it next year, OK?
25. QUANG	(KISSING HER) It's serious. I have to give in to you in every thing, haven't I?
26. NGAN	(GIGGLING) Managing a nation is more difficult than controlling a lady. It's natural to be the loser!
27. QUANG	Every thing is not settled yet, stop dreaming.... Wait and see who will be the winner!... Let's go home. Today, Aunt Chi from my homeland visits my house. My mother invites you to have lunch with my family.

28. MUSIC. BRIEF MUSIC TO CHANGE SCENE.

29. QUANG	Here we are ... Ngan ... when we are in front of my parents, don't talk about the research on drug abuse, which has been assigned to me.... It is the old people's characteristic to think too much, it will always bother them and they will talk a lot and ask us to do this or that...
30. NGAN	(PRETENDING TO THREATEN HIM) If you are not arrogant, I will keep silent. If not ... watch out!
31. QUANG	(GOING OFF) Come on then, let's go inside....

32. FX. CAR APPROACHING FROM DISTANCE. THEN STOPS. CAR DOOR BANGS

OVERCOMING CHALLENGE
Pilot Test—Audio Episode #1

33. MR. THEP	(COMING ON) Mr Loc, welcome. You too, Tien. Loyal members of my staff. Today, we welcome my wife's sister who has just arrived from her rural homeland. She has brought some rural special food. So please, come in and have lunch with my family.
34. MR. LOC	I'm ready, Mr Thep, sir.... But Tien is busy searching for a wife.
35. TIEN	You two, don't incite me to do foolish things.... I don't need women who never think deeply and who are flirtatious.... I know a group of unmarried men like me. We often meet on every Saturday and drink beer together, then come back home. No problem at all!
36. MR. THEP	(JOKINGLY) You behave like a bird which was hit by an arrow. So, next time it saw a curved branch it thought that it was the bow which is zeroing onto it. OK, go ahead! But come on (GOING OFF) Let's go inside and join the others.
37. DIEN	(RUNNING IN) Hi Dad. Good evening Uncle Loc.... Dad, look ... Look what I'm wearing.
38. MR. THEP	Why did you wear that, Dien?... It makes you look like a boy disguising himself a girl?
39. MR. LOC	Dien, you are going to be a teenager soon, you grow so quickly....
40. DIEN	Last year, when you came, Mr Loc, you also told me that I would be a teenager soon. This year, you said the same thing again ... I've grown up already.
41. MR. LOC	(LAUGHS) Oh, I forget, I'm sorry, Dien.
42. DIEN	I told Mum not to buy me a skirt, but Mum still bought it.... She said she wants me to be feminine. Why should I be feminine ... to be teased by boys?
43. MR. THEP	(LAUGHING) It will be much better if you are feminine but you are not harassed by boys.
44. DIEN	In my class, the girls are sniveling, whimsical and giving themselves very fine airs.... I don't like it. I want to be like Brother Quang.

45. MR. THEP	It means that I have two sons! I want you to be my daughter.
46. MRS. THEP	(IN DISTANCE) Dien, stop.... Let Uncle Loc and your Dad to come in and get ready for the lunch!
47. MR. THEP	(COMING IN) Ah, is it special pickle I see on the table? I know that whenever you come dear sister-in-law, you always bring with you this delicacy. It is very delicious! I have traveled a lot and eaten different foods. But nothing is as delicious as this one from my wife's homeland. And it will be more wonderful if it is made by aunt Chi.
48. MRS. THEP	You have a good mouth, husband, and no one can compete....
49. MRS. CHI	But ... I learned my cooking from my sister.... Here, these things from my house are wonderful. These vegetables were grown up in my garden. I use no chemical insecticide. You don't have to worry.
50. MR. LOC	It's true that every thing is now in danger. Everything is polluted. Vegetables are sprayed with chemical insecticide. Poultry are fed with food causing genetic change. The air is polluted. Water is mixed with substances.... Causing many diseases!
51. MR. THEP	Well.... Let's eat. This is clean food. Please, help yourself!
52. MR. THEP	(WHILE EATING) Quang, how is your work at the Youth Institute?
53. QUANG	Everything is fine, Dad! I have completed the probation period.
54. MR. THEP	(HAPPILY) Have you? Have you been assigned to be in charge of any research or are you still assistant to some scientific doctors or MAs?
55. QUANG	(HESITATING SLIGHTLY) Well, I have been assigned to conduct a research on a topic relating to the youth. It's ... um ... It is an easy task ... about social evils!
56. MR. THEP	What is it about?.... Well, Why don't you suggest to your leaders to research on the increase of gambling in the society today.

OVERCOMING CHALLENGE
Pilot Test—Audio Episode #1   Page 6 of 7

Many agencies allow their staff to play gambling during working hours.... It's unacceptable!

57. MR. LOC   To date, gambling is becoming a national problem. People even play gambling openly on the pavement.

58. QUANG   (CHANGING THE TOPIC) Talking about social evils, they are varied ... Ah, Sorry I forget to ask you.... When will be the contest for participants from the northern provinces, Mai?... I'm sure that my cousin Mai will win the contest's prize.

59. MAI   Don't put the heavy burden of much hope on my shoulder. I take part in the event in order to try to see how far I can go.

60. MR. THEP   You see, Mr Loc, my wife's family is going to have a famous singer. No one expected that a small girl called Mai who was so tiny and thin in the past would one day be able to sing wonderfully.

61. MR. LOC   I was told that this year's contest is really big. Is it true?

62. NGAN   Yes! This is also an opportunity to promote new singers. It's pity that I'm not assigned to write about the contest.

63. MRS. CHI   Please, don't make Mai feel embarrassed. It is natural for a mother to think that her daughter is the best, but in fact, there are many others who are much better....

64. MAI   Don't worry, Mother!... I'm not the type who has to win a prize at any price.

65. MRS. THEP   (LAUGHINGLY) Well. Please continue the meal. You all seem to think that I and my sister are not good cooks, because you only talk and don't eat anything?

66. MUSIC. BRIEF MUSIC TO CHANGE SCENE.

The translation of the script from video to audio continued in this manner. At the end of the episode, the Announcer was heard:

201.ANNOUNCER So ends today's episode of *Overcoming Challenge*. What sort of trouble is Quang getting into? Is he right to continue with his research even when the head of the Youth Research Institute has told him not to? And what about Ngan? Will she be in trouble, too, because of her association with Quang? Be sure to listen to the next episode to find out what happens with Quang and Ngan and all the other characters who are learning about overcoming challenge.

202. MUSIC. CLOSING MUSIC UP TO END.

PART 7

For All
Project Participants

13

MAJOR CHECKLIST

Photograph by Harvey Nelson

The program manager can establish a major checklist to help keep all aspects of the project on track.

THE IMPORTANCE OF THE MAJOR CHECKLIST

A project of the size and complexity of an Entertainment–Education TV serial drama can provide ample opportunity for problems to occur. One of the program manager's most important and most challenging tasks is to find and employ methods of *problem control*. Perhaps the most important first step in problem control is the establishment of a major checklist showing the essential steps and tasks to be accomplished. This checklist should be displayed prominently in the project office and all those involved with the project should become acquainted with those parts of the list that are their responsibility. What follows is a typical major checklist, but it should be remembered that the checklist for each project will be different from all others. The program manager and staff must determine all the details essential for the completion of their own project.

In the following checklist sample, the DONE column can be used for entering the date at which once-only activities have been completed (such as the conducting and analyzing of the pilot tests). The FOLLOW-UP column is used to record comments on how to bring a particular activity back on track, or other steps still to be undertaken to complete the activity.

Sample Major Checklist

	FOLLOW-UP	DONE
Preparation		
On air start-up date and overall project duration established.		
Choice of broadcast outlet (TV station) made.		
Contact made with other organizations (NGOs) engaged in similar projects to discuss how projects can work together.		

(Contd)

(*Contd*)

	FOLLOW-UP	DONE
Availability of resources for audience (e.g., contraceptives) determined.		
All necessary staff hired.		
Budget established.		
Production houses researched for adequate resources.		
Availability of local writing and acting talent explored.		
Possible frequency of broadcast and duration of each episode researched with broadcast outlet.		
Preliminary agreement reached with broadcast outlet, with regard to availability of time and estimates of cost.		
Design		
Date set for design workshop.		
Design workshop site chosen and reserved.		
Design team chosen and invited to design workshop.		
Preparations for design workshop completed.		
Design workshop held.		
Writer auditions completed; writer(s) chosen.		
Review panel selected. Initial review panel meeting held to outline responsibilities and review design document.		
Design document completed.		
Design document signing ceremony held (if required).		
Training needs established and training for writer(s) organized if needed.		
Pilot testing		
Pilot test sites selected and arranged.		
Pilot test dates established and pilot audiences invited for those dates.		
Story treatment (synopsis) and character profiles completed by writer.		
Story treatment and character profiles reviewed by review panel and adjusted by writer as necessary.		
Pilot episodes written.		

(*Contd*)

(Contd)

	FOLLOW-UP	DONE
Pilot support materials prepared (in audio version if necessary).		
Pilot test episodes and support materials reviewed.		
Pilot tests recorded.		
Pilot test questions prepared and reviewed.		
Pilot tests carried out (with writer/s present).		
Pilot test results compiled immediately after pilot tests.		
Pilot test results reviewed by program manager, writer, and review team.		
Decisions made with regard to changes to be incorporated in future scripts and support materials.		
Time line completed, agreed upon and shared with all who must abide by it.		

Writing
Writer visits audience and compiles detailed audience profiles to assist in story development.		
Regular meeting times established with writer, editor (where necessary), and director.		
Big board, other script monitoring device set up.		
Script page templates with headers, script cover pages, and review pages prepared.		
Writer training under way (as needed).		
Regular writing schedule established by writer. Episode writing begun.		
Regular review routine established.		
Regular routine established for typing, translation, and copying (as needed).		
Original music (if desired) commissioned and written, preferably in time to go with pilot episodes.		
Ongoing preparation of support materials is under way.		
Artwork for support and promotional materials commissioned.		
Promotional materials under development (making use of same musicians and artists as those used for episodes and support materials).		

(Contd)

(*Contd*)

	FOLLOW-UP	DONE
Contracts		
Production houses invited to submit proposals.		
Proposals examined and selection made.		
Production house contract prepared and approved.		
Production house contract signed.		
Writer contract(s) prepared and approved.		
Writer contract(s) signed.		
Actor (Artist) contracts prepared and approved (if these are separate from the production house).		
Actor (Artist) contracts signed.		
Research/evaluation team selected.		
Research/evaluation team contract prepared and approved.		
Research/evaluation contracts signed.		
Promotion Agency selected (if required).		
Promotion Agency contract prepared and approved.		
Promotion Agency contract signed.		
(Support materials might be prepared by the same agency that prepares the promotion materials. A separate contract will be needed for the Support Material developer unless these are to be developed in house).		
Production		
The following activities are carried out by the production house but should be monitored by the program manager.		
Shooting locations determined.		
Locations hired if necessary.		
Sets built, if necessary.		
All necessary shooting, sound recording, equipment on hand or ordered.		
Appropriate actors selected (and contracted).		
Editing facilities hired for appropriate dates (if needed).		
Message monitor appointed by the program manager, to attend all shoots.		
Director reviews and approves scripts.		

(*Contd*)

(Contd)

	FOLLOW-UP	DONE
Actors guided in the rules of Entertainment–Education acting.		
Time line for shooting and editing established.		
Program manager is notified of shooting and editing dates.		
Program manager attends several shoots to ensure accuracy and quality.		
Program manager attends editing sessions to ensure accuracy and quality.		
Finished episodes reviewed by program manager.		
Finished episodes delivered to broadcast outlet on time.		
Promotion and support		
Promotion campaign proposals discussed with and approved by program manager.		
Promotion campaign materials reviewed and approved by program manager.		
Promotion materials delivered to outlets on time.		
Support materials proposals discussed with and approved by program manager.		
Support materials pre-tested as necessary and adjusted.		
Support materials delivered to distribution points as needed.		
Where necessary, training provided in use of support materials.		
Monitoring and evaluation		
Ongoing monitoring designed.		
Monitoring sites and monitoring methods established.		
Monitoring begun and ongoing.		
Results of monitoring tabulated. Where necessary, changes recommended by the program manager to the writer for future episodes.		
Arrangements made for summative evaluation (post-tests).		

(Contd)

(*Contd*)

	FOLLOW-UP	DONE
Summative evaluation carried out.		
Results of summative evaluation compiled. Ongoing publicity and advocacy for the series.		
Reports prepared and distributed showing all aspects of project and its results and lessons learned.		
Arrangements made for continuation of the series if necessary (at least six months prior to end of current broadcast for a 52-episode serial and three months for a 26-episode serial).		

GUIDELINES FOR PREVENTING PROBLEMS AND MAINTAINING THE TIME LINE

1. **Allow sufficient start-up time:** At least six months—preferably more—should be allowed from the time of the decision to institute an Entertainment–Education serial drama project to the commencement of scriptwriting. This means six months of intense and continuous work, rather than doing a little bit about the project once a week or every few weeks. The tasks listed in Chapter 2 can be used as a guide to those things which must be accomplished within the first six months, but in every situation there will be extra tasks that need to be accomplished. The list is always longer—never shorter.

2. **Ensure that all personnel can work to the designated time line:** Remember—the very first time scriptwriting or reviewing or shooting falls behind the deadline, the program manager should discuss the problem with those concerned, and find a way of making it possible for the deficit to be made up. Permitting the time line to slip once without comment or concern is obvious encouragement for it to happen again.

3. **Encourage professionalism:** Professionalism should be encouraged in all those who are involved with the project, including writers, actors, and musicians. A big part of developing project sustainability is building a sense of personal professional pride in those engaged in the project. A bulletin board, displaying the "Professional of the Month" has been found beneficial in some projects. Similarly, an occasional one-day professional advocacy workshop can assist all those in the project to understand the meaning and value of professionalism and how to achieve it in their work.

Establishing professional contracts can also be helpful. The question of penalties or incentives often arises in the consideration of contracts related to the creation of Entertainment–Education serial drama. Decisions about whether or not to impose penalties for unmet contractual obligations can be made only on an individual project basis and in the context of local conditions. While the inclusion of penalties for late, incomplete, or below standard work certainly encourages professionalism, it is unacceptable in some cultures. If penalties are to be included in the contracts, then the program manager is under strong obligations to ensure that nothing on the project side makes it impossible or even difficult for contractors to live up to their obligations. The program manager should also take on the responsibility of being alert to any impending contract breaches and make efforts to assist the contractors to avoid incurring penalties, and encourage them to obtain the offered incentives.

4. **Discourage the practice of one person doing two major tasks:** It usually does not work well to have the same person undertake two major tasks, such as both the writing of the scripts and the directing of the shoot. Where there are two different people performing these tasks, one can keep professional pressure on the other. The director can hardly complain to the writer about late scripts if they are one and the same person!

5. **Arrange necessary training in advance:** As earlier chapters have suggested, possible areas for training are:

   - scriptwriting for Entertainment–Education serials
   - production
   - sound recording and mixing
   - TV acting

Sometimes it is necessary to bring in consultants for these training activities and it is as well to establish dates as far in advance as possible to ensure that consultants are available.

6. **Build FALL-BACK DAYS into the time line:** *For example*: If the time line allows for five weeks in which the writer should create 10 episodes and complete the revision of 10 earlier episodes, try adding—from the outset—a sixth week on the writer's schedule (in which there are no script requirements scheduled). Similarly, fall-back days can be added to the shooting schedule to allow for such problems as the illness of an actor or serious weather constraints.

   Project personnel should be persuaded never to use the fall-back days unless it is absolutely necessary and fully approved by the program manager. In this way a bank of spare time is built up that can accommodate more serious emergencies if they arise.

7. **Implement preparation steps whenever possible:** Ensure that all of the following preparations are made well in advance:

   - *Script cover sheets:* Templates for these can be completed and given to the writer even before pilot episode writing commences.
   - *Script page headers:* These should be stored in the computer ready for use when scripts are entered. For writers using a typewriter, it saves time and enhances accuracy to supply them with typing paper that has the headers already printed on them.
   - *Script review cover sheets:* These should be prepared so that they can be appended to each script that goes out for review.

8. **Order required materials ahead of time and in sufficient quantities:** If, for example, the project office is preparing script copies for the film production company, there will be a requirement of ample supplies of paper. Similarly, there might be other materials or supplies that will be needed in the office or on the set. The need for these things should be determined well in advance and orders placed in good time.

9. **Conduct the review panel meeting:** Before any script reviewing begins, a review panel meeting should be conducted so that all reviewers know exactly what their responsibilities are and exactly how to fill out the review sheets. The importance of the review panel to the success of the project should be stressed in the initial meeting, together with the essential nature of timely return of script review comments.

10. **Establish a practical script presentation format:** Writers and typists should be given clear guidelines on how the script should be presented on the printed page. This facilitates the work of the typists, the reviewers, the director, the technicians, and anyone else using the script. A sample of a recommended format for TV or film script presentation has been provided in Chapter 5.

11. **Conduct regular meetings** at which everyone working on the scripts: writer, director, translator, typist, language reviewer (if one is used), and script reviewers, can raise questions and concerns before serious difficulties arise. These meetings also provide a venue for the sharing of suggestions and ideas that can enhance the ongoing work of the project.

12. **Maintain the tracking system rigidly:** Once the continuous process of writing, reviewing, shooting, and editing is under way, the program manager must keep very close watch to be sure that quality is being maintained. The tracking system should be adhered to rigorously from Day 1 of the writing and production

cycle. The program manager might have to start out by checking the tracking system personally at the end of each day to be sure it has been completed. Once the routine has been established, an assistant can oversee the system and alert the program manager when something goes wrong.

13. **Be prepared for foreseeable difficulties:** There are some problems that are quite likely to arise in any long-running series. It is advisable to be aware of these and to give some thought to how they will be handled if they do arise. The most common problems that can occur in serial drama creation are:

- **Disability of a writer:** Have a back-up writer in mind. Where a writing team is being used, it is possible to call on the other writers to fill in briefly for the one who is absent. Where there is one writer working alone, the program manager should be aware of someone who can take over temporarily at short notice if needed. This might be someone on the project staff who has writing ability and has been reviewing the scripts regularly. Alternatively, it is wise to be aware of one or two other writers who could be called upon if the primary writer has to drop out of the job permanently. Give the new writer all previously written scripts and a copy of the design document, and allow two weeks before submission of some new scripts. This is an obvious place where fall-back time will be invaluable.

- **Disability of an actor:** This can cause considerable disruption if episodes are being shot very close to broadcast date. If there is a reasonable time lapse between writing, production, and broadcast, it is much easier to ask the writer to write out a particular character for a certain time, or indeed, if necessary, to remove the character from the story altogether. Alternatively, it might be better to re-shoot all scenes in which the incapacitated actor appeared, using a new actor. If the actor has the part of a character who is vital to the drama, the best approach is to write into the drama a storyline that has the character go on a trip, or become ill. In this way, you can leave the character out of the drama for several episodes, and then have a new actor take over the role at a later time. Some directors even recommend informing the audience that a new actor will be taking over at a certain date.

    Other problems, such as electricity shortages, strikes, and political disturbances are not so easy to prepare for in advance. The biggest asset to overcoming problems of any type is keeping all aspects of the project rigidly on the time line and maintaining some fall-back time when there are no problems occurring.

14. **Know and use major checklists:** Everyone involved with the project should be aware of the multitude of steps that must be accomplished satisfactorily—many of them on a continuing basis—if the project is to reach its goal. Some program managers like to display prominently and permanently a checklist similar to the one at the beginning of this chapter to encourage staff to appreciate the value of everyone completing tasks on time and the necessity of maintaining professional standards.

15. **Stress Q and A at all times:** Quality **(Q)** and Accuracy **(A)** are essential if the Entertainment–Education drama is to have a positive effect on the lives of the audience.

Preparing for the Design Workshop

SAMPLE INVITATION LETTERS

The following are suggestions for letters of invitation that could be sent to those chosen to be members of the Design Team.

For Content Specialists

Dear

(Name your organization) in association with the (name of sponsoring agency such as a local government agency or an international agency like UNICEF or the Packard Foundation or the United States Agency for International Development) is preparing to create a television drama serial (or film, etc., as appropriate) to encourage (name your topic).

In order to ensure that the messages delivered through the drama serial are accurate and appropriate, we are holding a Design Workshop at (name the venue) from (opening date) to (closing date). We would very much appreciate your presence as a Design Team member for the full duration of this workshop.

The aim of this workshop is to prepare a Design Document which will contain the **exact messages** that must be contained in each of the episodes of the drama serial. Your contribution to developing these messages would be very welcome. We would like to have your assurance that you can be with us for the entire workshop so that we can be sure that all Design Team members have the opportunity to discuss and agree upon all contents of the Design Document.

It would be most helpful if you could bring with you any print or other materials relevant to our main topic so that you can share the most up-to-date knowledge with other team members during our small group work.

The Design Workshop will open with a dinner on (name the date) at (name the venue) to which you are cordially invited. Then the workshop will run each day from (opening time) to (closing time). Please see attached agenda.

(*Information such as the following can be added as appropriate:*)

Board and food will be provided for you throughout the workshop and you will receive a per diem of _____.

Invitation for Writers

(Name your organization) in association with (name your funding agency) is preparing to create a television drama serial (or film, etc., as appropriate) to encourage (specify topic).

In order to ensure that the messages delivered through the drama serial are accurate and appropriate, we are holding a Design Workshop at (name the venue) from (opening date) to (closing date). We would very much appreciate your presence as a Design Team member for the duration of this workshop.

The aim of this workshop is to prepare a Design Document which will contain the **exact messages** that must be contained in each of the episodes of the drama serial. Your contribution to developing these messages and ensuring their appropriateness would be very welcome. We would like to have your assurance that you can be with us for the entire workshop so that we can be sure that all Design Team members have a chance to discuss and agree on all the contents of the Design Document.

In your role as a possible writer for this drama, we believe that you will benefit greatly by being part of The Design Team and taking part in the determination of the message content. We would hope that by the end of the workshop week, you will be able to start preparing some possible story-lines and character profiles that could be used for the drama serial. We would like to encourage you to think of ways of creating an exciting, culturally appropriate story that would allow our messages to be brought in naturally and gradually and subtly. You will have the opportunity to meet with representatives of our chosen audience, as well as with the content (or message) specialists. This will help you to understand the audience's likes and needs, and also to gain a clear under-standing of the messages that are to be incorporated into your story.

The Design Workshop will open with a dinner on (name the date) at (name the venue) to which you are cordially invited. Then the workshop will run each day from (opening time) to (closing time). Please see attached agenda.

(*Information such as the following can be added as appropriate.*)

Board and food will be provided for you throughout the workshop and you will receive a per diem of _____.

DESIGN WORKSHOP NEEDS

For Facilitators

- Flip charts × 2
- Flip chart pens: two sets of three colors
- Sticky stuff for attaching paper to walls
- Computer for Power Point presentations
- Overhead projector
- Overhead transparencies (for use by participants)
- Transparency pens and erasers
- Stapler and staples
- Table(s) for facilitator's materials
- File cards
- Pens, pencils, rulers
- Scissors

For Computer Operator (Stenographer)

- Computer for compiling completed message pages
- Printer
- Copier
- Copy paper

For Participants

- Agenda
- Notebooks
- Pens
- Name tags to put on the tables in front of them and/or to wear on their lapels
- Copies of support materials (at least enough for one copy per small working group)
- Copies of this book, that team members can use as a guide during their work
- Copies of research report used for Justification presentation

For Plenary Session Room

- Tables and chairs—set in U-shape facing front
- Wastepaper baskets

- Tissues
- Water

For Small Group Work

- Separate small meeting rooms OR
- A plenary session room that can be easily modified for small group work
- Copies of Message Content pages (see next page); Be sure there are enough for the number of episodes (i.e., 26, 52, etc.) plus some extras.
- Video tape player and videos for screening sample(s) of Entertainment–Education videos.

SAMPLE MESSAGE PAGE

To be filled in by groups as they prepare the message(s) for each episode of the drama:

Episode

Topic:
Sub Topic:

Measurable Objectives: After this episode, the audience will

KNOW:

DO:

HAVE AN ATTITUDE OF:

PURPOSES:
The purposes of this episode are:

    To _____.
    To _____.
    To _____ (*and so on, as needed*).

CONTENT:
(Content can be continued on the back of this page if extra room is needed)

GLOSSARY:

SCRIPT EVALUATION SHEET

One copy to be completed by each Design Team member, for each story outline presented by the auditioning writers at the Design Workshop.

STORY TITLE: _____

WRITER'S NAME: _____

1. What is the format of this drama: ☐ Serial   ☐ Series   ☐ Stand-alone film
2. How well do you think this story would appeal to our audience(s)?
   ☐ A lot   ☐ A bit   ☐ Not very much
3. Do you think this story will allow our messages to come in comfortably?
   ☐ Yes   ☐ No

Explain your answer:
_____

_____

4. Name or briefly describe TWO of the characters in the story, who you think would interest the audience:

_____

_____

_____

5. Is there any humor in the story outline? ☐ Yes   ☐ No
   If so, which character provides the humor?
   Is the humor appropriate to the audience and the story? ☐ Yes   ☐ No
6. Briefly explain your opinion of this story outline and why you think it would be or would not be suitable for our purposes:

_____

_____

_____

_____

If you like the outline, but you would like to recommend any important changes, please write your comments here and/or on the other side of this page.

_____

_____

_____

_____

_____

7C SAMPLES

The Program Manager might like to share the following examples with the Design Team and with the Review Team to give them a clear understanding of the importance of the 7Cs of message presentation.

Invite team members to examine each of the following examples and suggest how they would improve them:

- Is this **Correct?**

  Exclusive breastfeeding for the first six months of the baby's life will ensure good health for the baby.

This is a false promise.

- Is this **Complete?**

  To ensure proper growth, make sure your child is given a balanced diet every day.

*This is too vague. What is a balanced diet? Also, the balanced diet varies according to the child's **age** group.*

- If a woman is infected with HIV when she becomes pregnant or during pregnancy, she should get medical help. With proper care, the child can be protected from the disease and lead a healthy life.

This is a difficult situation. The statement does not explain that the child is very likely to be left an orphan, because while the child might be protected with medication, the mother will not and might die before the child grows up.

- Is this **Clear (and/or logical)?**

  Your baby must be fully immunized within the first year of life. Be sure to find out from your Health Provider when to bring your baby to the clinic for the appropriate vaccinations.

Using both words—"immunization" and "vaccination"—can be confusing for many parents.

  HIV can be passed to another person through infected blood. This could happen through using infected needles, tattooing with dirty equipment or sharing dirty razors.

*The problem here is the question of **how** someone will know if the needles etc. have been used by a person who is infected with HIV.*

  Stay healthy by using the ABCs: Abstinence, Being faithful, or always using Condoms when having sex.

*Here, the audience is faced with the problem: How can a couple become pregnant if they **always** use condoms while having sex?*

- Is this **Consistent?**

   The Intrauterine Device (IUD) cannot move around in the woman's body.
   The IUD can slip out of the vagina, so the woman must check the string every month to be sure the device is still in place.

*The second statement seems to contradict the first. An audience hearing this on radio or television could be forgiven for thinking the first statement said the IUD **could** move around in the woman's body.*

- Is this **Culturally appropriate?**
   Adolescent girls can go to the clinic to learn more about how to protect themselves from unwanted pregnancy.

In many countries, this would be very bad advice to give on television or radio. In some places young girls are not encouraged—or even allowed—to go to a clinic by themselves because people seeing them there would assume they had already "done something wrong" like becoming pregnant or contracting an STI.

- Is this **Compelling?**

   Women are necessary in the world, so female fetuses should not be aborted before birth.

This is a statement of fact, but it is hardly likely to compel men to ensure that their wives are properly cared for during pregnancy.

- Is this **Concise?**

The following extract is taken from a Design Document for a series of programs for a general rural audience. There is far too much detail to fit comfortably into one program, and more than is needed to encourage the use of the pill. The content should be reduced to no more than 10 lines. Reviewers can practice the skill of being concise by considering how they would reduce this content to 10 lines.

- Oral pill is a temporary contraceptive method used by women. The oral pill is taken by a woman daily to prevent pregnancy.
- A woman should use the oral pill to prevent pregnancy ONLY after she has visited a service provider to make sure the pill is suitable for her.
- It is highly effective when taken daily and is perfectly safe.
- It can be taken regularly for a long time in accordance with the Health Service Provider's advice.
- Advantages

   - It is convenient and easy to use.
   - The woman can conceive immediately after she stops the pill.

- Many women taking the pill find their periods come regularly every month, they have less menstrual cramps and less bleeding.
- It prevents pregnancy for as long as the woman wants if she continues taking the pills.

- When to start taking the pill

  - Go to your health provider to understand when you should start taking the pill.

- How to take the pill

  - When a service provider recommends the oral pill, ask him/her for all the details on how to take it correctly.
  - All you have to do is take the pill at the same time every day. Select a time that suits you, such as at bedtime. The pill has to be taken irrespective of sexual activity every day.

- When you miss taking the pill

  - If you miss it one day, take the missed pill at once and take the regular pill for that day as well at the usual time.
  - If you miss taking pills on two days, take two pills on the next two days, followed by one pill everyday. Also use condoms for the next seven days and contact your health service provider.
  - The pill is highly effective when taken correctly. Women should and can find out all details on how to use the pill correctly from the health service provider. Taking the pill may create certain temporary changes within the body in some women. The Health Service Provider will provide all the information you need to decide if the pill is the right method for you.

- Where to get the pill?

  - The pills are available from the service provider, at the health center and in the market.
  - If the woman is using the oral contraceptive pill, her husband should support her by making sure she takes the pill regularly every day.
  - A well-planned family offers every family member the chance of a better life. Using the oral contraceptive pill is an easy way to space children and have a small family.

Design Document Sample Pages

These pages are extracted from a Design Document prepared in Uganda for a 13-part TV series

---

DESIGN DOCUMENT
FOR
A 13-PART ENTERTAINMENT–EDUCATION
TELEVISION SERIES

PREPARED BY THE
DESIGN TEAM OF DISH II PROJECT TELEVISION SERIES
DESIGN DOCUMENT WORKSHOP

HELD AT
HOTEL TRIANGLE ANNEX
JINJA

TABLE OF CONTENTS

On this page, the document presented a full table of contents, followed by a Participant List, giving the names of all those who had been part of the design team, and the organizations they represented. The document then continued as follows:

Part 1: Background and Overall Description

1. Justification

Background

A primary objective of the Delivery of Improved Services of Health II (DISH II) Project in Uganda is to improve critical maternal, child and reproductive health behavior among families and communities in 12 districts of Uganda within the next two years. Improved health practices that the project will promote are: family planning, maternal health, infant nutrition, male involvement in family planning, HIV counseling and testing, prevention of mother to child transmission (PMTCT), treatment and prevention of sexually transmitted infections (STIs), immunization, child health, and utilization of quality health services.

The project will accomplish this through a combination of phased multi-channel communication campaigns. There will be a quarterly newsletter entitled *Health Matters*, a weekly television series, and a weekly radio series. These media will tie together messages from several campaigns and will continue to reinforce messages from past campaigns as new campaigns are launched.

Multi-channel campaigns will be launched in the following sequence:

Year 1: Male involvement in family planning, infant nutrition
Year 2: Home management of fever/malaria in children, immunization, safe motherhood, long
term and permanent methods (LTPM) of family planning, adolescent reproductive health
Year 3: Transmission and prevention of HIV, and promotion of quality health care services

The centerpiece television series will emphasize these messages while the campaigns are at their peak; and will continue to carry these messages after the intensive campaign activities have subsided.

Background research
Reproductive, Maternal and Child Health Issues
Intensive background research on the topics of this project reveal the following facts:

Infant nutrition

- More than 30 percent of 3-year-olds are stunted.
- Stunting caused by chronic poor intake of food.

- Stunting begins during first 2 years of life, when parents have control over babies' diets.
- Less than one quarter of mothers exclusively breastfeed for the first 6 months.
- Most parents do not add adequate quantities of complementary foods at 6 months.

Long-term and permanent family planning (FP) methods

- 11 per cent of women want to stop childbearing but are not using family planning.
- Permanent methods: Tubal ligation and vasectomy acceptance has not been increasing as rapidly as other methods.
- Many men and women fear these permanent FP methods.
- Norplant is relatively unknown.
- All these methods are more widely available than in previous years, but still not widely used.

Adolescent reproductive health

- By the age of 19 years more than 70 per cent of girls are sexually active.
- Almost 50 per cent of women become pregnant before the age of 18.
- One-third of all maternal deaths are among adolescents.
- Most new HIV infections occur among 15–19-year-olds.
- Adolescents shy away from health facilities, even when they have problems.

Mother to child HIV transmission

- 30 per cent of babies born to HIV positive mothers become infected.
- All babies born to HIV positive mothers become orphans.
- Few mothers or fathers know the facts about mother to child transmission of HIV.

Safe motherhood

- Maternal mortality among the highest in world.
- Neonatal mortality among the highest in world.
- Only about 30 per cent of women deliver at health facility.
- Most deaths due to sepsis, prolonged labor, or hemorrhage.
- Cultural beliefs stop women from visiting ANC centers regularly or delivering in health centers.

Immunization

- In DISH II districts, complete immunization is only 34 percent, and has been declining.
- Main reasons for low immunizations are ignorance, and fear that immunization is dangerous.

Male involvement in family health

- Men see themselves as authority figures but don't often discuss family health with wives.
- Men know less about modern FP methods than women.
- Men usually control money for health care.

Quality of care

- Quality of care has been improving.
- Community perceives services as still poor.
- Service providers feel unappreciated.
- Service providers want to do a good job.
- New strategy now in place to improve and maintain basic standards of care.

2. Television Series Audience

Primary audience

- Men and women 15–35 years old living in rural areas and trading centers.

Secondary audience

- Health providers, opinion leaders, older women, mothers and mothers-in-law of primary audience.

Audience analysis

At this point, the design document contained detailed analysis on the lifestyles of the various audience groups, together with information about their TV viewing habits. Then, for each of the topics to be covered in the series, the design team collected and noted important audience information, such as the following:

Audience analysis in terms of series messages

A. CONTRACEPTIVE: VASECTOMY

An examination of the current reluctance among Ugandan couples to opt for vasectomy indicates:

Cause of current behavior

- Fear of loss of manhood by both the men and women.

How fear can be removed

- Provide relevant knowledge about the method
- Testimonies from credible satisfied clients
- Information about where services are available and where they can obtain information

Change Agents (Motivators)

- Satisfied users
- Service providers

B. TUBAL LIGATION

- An examination of the current reluctance among Ugandan couples to opt for tubal ligation indicates:

Cause of current behavior

- Women fear becoming weak and unable to perform their duties.

How fear can be removed

- Testimonies from credible satisfied clients
- Relevant knowledge about tubal ligation

Change Agents (Motivators)

- Satisfied users
- Service providers

C. NORPLANT

An examination of the current reluctance among Ugandan couples to opt for Norplant contraceptive indicates:

Cause of current reluctance to use Norplant

- Lack of awareness about the method.
- Belief that it travels in the body and that the arm becomes weak.

What can be done to change belief

- Provide relevant knowledge

Change Agents (Motivators)

- Partners
- Satisfied users
- Service providers

D. SAFE MOTHERHOOD

Cause of mothers' reluctance to deliver at health facilities or return for post-natal care:

- Fear of poor handling at health facility by service providers.
- Delivery perceived to be a normal process—no risk.

What can be done to change behavior

- Demonstrate the ideal situation in a delivery unit at a health facility.
- Inform couples about the risks during pregnancy, delivery and post-natal period.
- Health providers should share information about pregnancy risks at community meetings.

Change Agents (Motivators)

- Service providers
- Community leaders
- Partners/in-laws

E. MALARIA

The problem

- Poor home management of malaria in children.
- High incidence of malaria among pregnant women.

Causes

- Misconceptions on the cause of malaria (many believe eating mangoes and maize causes malaria).
- Late initiation of treatment.
- Non-completion of dosage.
- Taking/using inappropriate medication.
- Not using insecticide treated materials (ITMs); e.g., mosquito nets.
- Not seen as a serious illness.
- Inability to recognize malaria/fever in children.
- Lack of awareness about chemoprophylaxis during pregnancy.
- Fear among pregnant women of taking malaria medication.
- Ignorance about risks to mother and baby associated with malaria.
- Miscarriage is not associated with malaria. It is attributed to infidelity and syphilis.

What can be done to change behavior

- Educate parents about the dangers, prevention, and treatment of malaria among children and pregnant women.
- Educate parents on how to recognize fever/malaria in children and how to treat it correctly.
- Educate couples about protecting house and family from malaria.

Change Agents (Motivators)

- Elders (mothers-in-law, aunties, traditional midwives, traditional healers)
- Health workers
- Community leaders (LCs, Opinion leaders)
- Mothers who manage malaria correctly

The analysis continued until all main topics had been covered.

3. Justification for the Chosen Medium: Television

- Television/video has been chosen for this series because it is important that some of these topics are demonstrated visually.
- Television/video is popular with people throughout Uganda. Video vans can bring Entertainment–Education programs to people in rural areas where videos are very popular.
- Television/video reaches approximately one quarter of women and almost one half of men in the country. Many are policymakers and opinion leaders.
- Television is expensive to produce, but the programs can be re-used many times.

4. Measurable Objectives of the Series Overall

As a result of these programs there will be a measurable increase in the number of male and female audience members who:

- Believe it is possible to protect themselves and their families from serious health problems.
- Talk with others about the healthy practices discussed in the programs.
- Seek information from health providers about these practices.
- Trust health providers and rely on their advice.
- Practice, as appropriate, healthy behavior as discussed in the programs.

5. Purposes of the Series Overall

- **To educate** the audience about basic ways to protect the health of themselves and their families.
- **To demonstrate** that the quality of health services throughout the country is improving and that health providers are competent and caring people.
- **To motivate** the audience to discuss protective health practices with others, and to seek more information from health providers.
- **To encourage** the audience to adopt relevant health practices.

6. Overall Message and Emotional Focus of the Series

The **Overall Message** to be transmitted through this series is:
Adopting healthy habits and practices and trusting the advice of health providers can help you ensure good health for yourself and all members of your family.
The predominant **emotions** to be shown in the drama are: **Love** for your family will inspire you to improve their health. You can have **pride** in a healthy family and **peace of mind** about their health.

7. The Number of Programs in the Series

There will be 13 programs in this series. This is equal to one quarter of a year, at the rate of one program per week.

8. The Duration of Each Program

Each program will be 25 minutes long, to fit into a 30-minute TV broadcast slot.

9. Series Format

The 13 programs will constitute a drama series, with each drama featuring the same main characters and taking place in the same location, but involved in a new "story" each week. The series will involve the people who work at Health Center IV in a busy rural trading centre in Uganda, and the clients they care for. Individual programs will be able to stand alone and will be shown in community settings. At the end of each program, a narrator will summarize the main message points of the program.

10. Sequence of Program Topics

1. Quality of care
2. Sanitation
3. Safe motherhood I: Protection from risks during labor and delivery
4. Malaria I: Home management of health for children
5. Family planning I: Norplant
6. Immunization
7. Mother to child HIV transmission
8. Adolescent reproductive health
9. Safe motherhood II: Post-natal care for mother and child
10. Infant nutrition
11. Malaria II: Controlling malaria during pregnancy
12. STI management
13. Family planning: Voluntary surgical contraception

Part 2: Message Content for Individual Programs

PROGRAM 1: QUALITY OF CARE (*No.1 of 1 for this topic*)

Measurable objectives: After this program, the audience will:

KNOW:

- Quality of care at health facilities is improving.
- Community involvement will make the services at health facilities even better.
- Providers care about and respect their clients and are willing to serve them.

DO:

- Go to the health facility and use services.
- Find out what they can do to help improve and maintain the health facility and the services and give what help they can.
- Believe health services are for their benefit and share this knowledge with others.

HAVE AN ATTITUDE OF:

Pride in their health facility.

PURPOSE:

The purposes of this program are:

- To inform the audience about improving quality services at health facilities in Uganda.
- To motivate them to play an active role in improving and maintaining the quality of services at their health facilities.

CONTENT:

The Ministry of Health is working to improve the quality of services at public health facilities throughout the country by:

- Setting standards and supervising the health facilities regularly and empowering the community to help maintain standards at the health facilities.
- Providing basic equipment/drugs.
- Maintaining facility infrastructure.
- Ensuring providers use safe procedures and practices.
- Ensuring health facilities have at least the minimum staffing levels.
- Ensuring that providers are trained, competent and committed to providing client-friendly services.

Members of the community should do what they can to assist the staff at the health facility to maintain the facility in good condition and to encourage others to make appropriate use of the health facility.

Community members can establish a Community Health Committee to monitor the health facility to ensure that it adheres to set standards. The Health Committee can also encourage all community members—including fathers and husbands—to learn about available services at the facility and ensure that all family members obtain health services when needed.

PROGRAM 2: SANITATION: HAND WASHING (*No. 1 of 1 for this topic*)

Measurable objectives: After this program, the audience will:

KNOW:

- That several diseases, like diarrhea and worm infection result from inappropriate sanitation in the home; especially failure to wash hands.

DO:

- Begin to always wash hands before preparing, serving, or eating food and after using a toilet/latrine.
- Encourage others in the family and the community to always wash hands on these occasions.

HAVE AN ATTITUDE OF:

- Pride in knowing that by washing their hands at the right time, they are contributing to the health of all family members.

PURPOSE:

The purposes of this program are:

- To educate the audience on the health risks of not washing hands.
- To motivate the audience to always wash their hands before preparing, serving, eating food and after using a latrine/toilet.

CONTENT:

- Germs that cause diarrhea and intestinal worms are present all around us. These germs are too small to see. Even if hands look clean, they might be carrying these dangerous germs.

- To protect your family against these diseases, ALWAYS wash your hands, preferably with soap and clean water:

  - Before preparing, serving, or eating food, and after using a toilet/latrine
  - after disposing of feces, including children's
  - after touching dirty things like rubbish

The simple act of making sure that all family members wash their hands with soap and water in these circumstances will go a long way in ensuring that everyone in the family has a better chance of staying healthy.

PROGRAM 3: SAFE MOTHERHOOD: PROTECTION FROM RISKS DURING LABOR AND DELIVERY (*No. 1 of 2 for this topic*):

Measurable objectives: After this program, the audience will:

KNOW:

- Risks during labor and delivery.
- Benefits of delivering at a health facility.

DO:

- Plan to deliver at a health facility.
- Encourage others to deliver at a health facility.

HAVE AN ATTITUDE OF:

- Belief that health facilities provide good quality services during labor and delivery and pride in being able to ensure safety for the mother and baby.

PURPOSE:

The purposes of this program are:

- To educate the audience about risks involved during labor and delivery.
- To encourage couples to have their babies delivered at a health facility.
- To demonstrate good care provided by service providers during labor and delivery.

CONTENT:

- Every birth is a special and joyous occasion, but every labor and delivery carries risks. A labor which starts as normal can become complicated at any stage of the process.

- The problems that may occur during labor and delivery include heavy bleeding, infection, prolonged labor, fits, and many others. Any one of these can lead to death of the mother or baby or both.
- Most of these problems cannot be treated in a home. Serious complication can be avoided, however, if pregnant women are taken to a health facility as soon as they start labor. At the health facility, help can be given immediately if any problems occur during labor or delivery.
- Midwives and doctors at the health facility are fully trained to manage problems that may arise during childbirth.
- Husbands and wives should discuss where the woman will deliver and make plans for getting her there as soon as labor begins.
- The health facility encourages women to bring a friend or relative to be with them during labor, while the midwife will make the woman as comfortable as possible.
- Women may use herbs on their bodies, but the midwife will not allow them to eat herbs or to insert them inside their private parts. This can be dangerous to the baby or the mother.
- Many women who have delivered at heath facilities have greatly appreciated the kind and competent care they have received. Many lives have been saved when women have given birth at a health facility.

Note to the writer:

- The program should include a demonstration of a midwife or doctor caring for a woman in labor at the health facility in a professional and caring manner.

The same detailed outline was provided for each of the other programs in the series.

The Design Document also provided a GLOSSARY which gave the local language interpretation of important technical words, and the following Acronym List.

Sample Acronym List

AIC	AIDS Information Centre
AIDS	Acquired Immune Deficiency Syndrome
AVSC	Association for Voluntary Surgical Contraception
ANC	Ante-natal care
BCC	Behavior Change Communication
DDHS	District Director of Health Services
DHE	District Health Educator
DISH	Delivery of Improved Services for Health Project
HIV	Human Immuno Deficiency Virus
IEC	Information, education and communication
IMCI	Integrated management of childhood illnesses
ITMs	Insecticide treated materials

LTPM	Long-term and permanent methods of family planning
LCs	Local Councillors
MOH	Ministry of health
PNC	Post-natal care
RH	Reproductive Health; this includes family planning, prevention and treatment of STDs, ante-natal and post-natal care, and counseling about HIV/AIDS
STIs	Sexually Transmitted Infections—now the preferred term for Sexually Transmitted Diseases (STDs)—are infections which are transmitted from one person to another during sexual intercourse

Production Budget Samples

Showing items to be considered in preparing the production budget:

Pre-production

1. (location hunting/ Artist selection & workshop with local people)
2. Stationery and office expenditure

Sub-total ....

Sub-total Pre-Production ....

Production

Shooting days = 20 days (3 locations)

1. Equipment hire:
   A. Camera/ sound × 20 days (includes monitor, microphone, etc.)
   B. Light:
      Multy 20: 2 PC × 15 days
      Multy 10: 5 PC × 15 days
      Baby solar: 3 PC × Rs 15 days
   C. Petrol generator 500 wt × 20 days
   D. Trolley × 15 days
   E. Reflector: 5 PC × 20 days
   F. Extension cable, board & socket
   G. Cutter stand 4 PC × 15 days
   H. Reflector paper/Black paper/Butter paper and Clips

Sub-total Production ....

2. Manpower:
   Cameraman × 20 days
   Soundman × 20 days
   Camera caretaker × 20 days
   Production Assist. × 20 days
   Make-up man × 20 days

Porter/Helper × 3 persons × 10 days
Light boys 3 persons × 15 days
Spot boys 2 persons × 20 days

Sub-total ....

3. Transportation: Land/Airfare (both locations)

Sub-total ....

4. Shooting Expenditure:
Lodge for 15 people × 22 days
Food & Tea 20 people × 22 days
Props
Costume
Make-up kit
Location charge

Sub-total ....

5. Artist Remuneration (local):
3 main artists
2 supporting artists
6 supporting artists (lesser roles)
Crowd and extras (two separate locations)

Sub-total ....
Sub-total Production ....

Post-production

1. Editing table hire: Logging & off-line editing
   Editor
2. Editing table: × 25 hr.
   Editor
3. Animation Graphics/titles
4. Music Recording/Studio 10 hr.
   Music Composition and Director
   Musician 8 persons
5. Sound Mix & transfer Master copy × 2 hr.
6. Sub-master copy × 1 hr.
7. VHS copy PAL 10 PC
8. VHS 10 SONY pro X PAL × 10 PC.

Sub-total ....

Manpower

1. Script Supervisor/continuity person 25 days
2. Assistant Director 30 days
3. Director 30 days

Sub-total ....
Sub-total Post-Production ....
GRAND TOTAL FOR VIDEO ....

Contract Samples

ARTIST/ACTOR

MEMORANDUM OF AN AGREEMENT
made and entered into by and between:

MEDIA FOR DEVELOPMENT TRUST (W.O. 21/89)
(hereinafter known as MFD)
and

_____
(hereinafter known as "the artist")

Whereas it is agreed that MFD engages the artist and the artist accepts the engagement to play the role of _____ in a feature film (hereinafter known as "the film") to be made by MFD and for the time being entitled _____ upon and subject to the following terms and conditions:

1. The artist agrees to make himself/herself available to MFD for the entirety of the workshop, during the period of _____ to _____; on any date during the period _____ through to _____ for rehearsals; and during the period _____ through _____ for shooting.
2. For the artist's services hereunder MFD shall pay to the artist as salary the sum of Zimbabwe $_____ for the whole of the period of their services to MFD.
3. The artist's salary shall be paid in installments as follows:

   10 per cent on signing this agreement.
   Balance on satisfactory completion of the filming of the artist's role.

4. The services of the artist shall be exclusive to MFD during the period of the first call aforementioned.

5. For the purposes of this Agreement a working day shall mean a period not exceeding 12 consecutive hours (breaks to include 1 hour's break for rest and refreshment).

6. The artist shall keep MFD informed of their whereabouts during the whole period of their engagement and shall not go and remain beyond 75 km distance from the studios or locations during that period of first call without MFD's consent.

7. MFD shall make arrangements for transport to and from a mutually agreed upon meeting place to the location during shooting. The artist however shall be responsible for arranging to attend rehearsals in the City himself/herself.

8. The artist agrees that they will not grant any interview to the press or to any other person discussing or dealing with the administration or policy of MFD or their present or future engagement with MFD nor shall the artist disclose or exchange any information about the film, the script or characters or production or its pre-production and research with the public either verbally or in writing without the specific permission of MFD in writing.

9. The artist shall not without the written consent of MFD incur any liabilities on behalf of MFD nor pledge MFD's credit.

10. The artist shall not be entitled to any royalties whatsoever nor share of any earnings gross or net received by MFD for the film from its distribution, or sale or any other benefit of any kind derived from the film, other than the salary referred to in this contract.

11. The artist agrees to render their services as and when required by MFD after completion of the shooting of their part in the film for purpose of retakes, extra scenes, post-synchronizing, recording, dubbing, the making of soundtracks and stills and otherwise for the purpose of completing the film.

12. MFD may at its discretion omit the artist from the film and in such event MFD shall have no liability to the artist in respect thereof save to pay to the artist the salary payable in respect of the part undertaken by the artist in terms of this Agreement.

SIGNED at HARARE this _____ day of _____ (month and year) in the presence of the undersigned witness.

AS WITNESS: AS WITNESS:

....

....

Media for Development Trust   ·   **Artist**

CREW MEMBER CONTRACT SAMPLE

MEMORANDUM OF AN AGREEMENT
made and entered into by and between:

MEDIA FOR DEVELOPMENT TRUST (W.O. 21/89)
and

_____

(hereinafter called "the crew-member") of the other part.

Whereas it is agreed that MFD engages the crew member and the crew member accepts the engagement to perform the duties of _____ in a motion picture (hereinafter called "the film") to be made by MFD and for the time being entitled "DISTRESS" upon and subject to the following terms and conditions:

Now therefore these Present Witness:

1. The period of engagement by MFD of the crew member shall commence on the _____ day of _____ 20 _____ and shall continue until the completion by the crew member of his duties hereunder as required by MFD.
2. While the duration of the shoot is anticipated to be for a period of six weeks, this may be reduced or extended at the discretion of MFD. In the event of any reduction of the duration of employment, MFD will advise the crew member of this at least one week in advance.
3. MFD shall pay the crew member in his capacity aforesaid a salary in the sum of Zimbabwe $ —— per —— for the crew member's services to MFD.
4. The crew member's salary shall be paid by MFD as follows:

    (a) in installments as follows:
    (b) weekly, not later than each Saturday during the period of the engagement in respect of the preceding week or part of a week ending on Saturday inclusive;

5. The crew member warrants and undertakes that he/she is at liberty to enter into this Agreement and he/she will perform his/her services hereunder to the best of his/her ability and in accordance with the instructions of MFD and MFD agrees to pay to the crew member in consideration of such services the sums aforementioned by way of remuneration.
6. (a) For the purposes of this Agreement a working day shall mean a period not exceeding 12 consecutive hours (breaks to include 1 hour's break for rest and refreshment).

    (b) The crew member shall, if so required, attend at the Studios or on location not more than 1 hour before the commencement of the working day for the purpose of assisting in the preparations for the day's shooting.

    (c) MFD will make arrangements for the crew member's transportation to and from a mutually agreed upon meeting place to the location during shooting. The crew member however shall be responsible for arranging to attend at the studio hired or in use by MFD in the City him/herself.

7. The crew member shall keep MFD informed of his/her whereabouts during the whole period of his/her engagement and shall not go and remain beyond 75 km distance from the studios or location during the currency of this agreement without MFD's consent.

8. The crew member shall be available to assist and render services as and when required by MFD, even after completion of the shooting of the film for the purpose of retakes, extra scenes, recording, dubbing, or otherwise, as the case may be, for the purpose of completing the film to the satisfaction of MFD.

9. The crew member agrees that he/she will:

    (a) render his/her services hereunder to the best of his/her ability in such manner as the company may direct.

    (b) be present as and when required at such studios or locations as MFD may direct at the time indicated.

    (c) comply with all the regulations of the studios or location in particular to refrain from consuming liquor during working hours and, where specifically required comply with any "no smoking" regulation in the studios or on location as well as all reasonable instructions that MFD may give for the production and proper conduct of the film.

    (d) not without the consent of MFD grant any interview to the press or to any other person discussing or dealing with the administration or policy of MFD or his/her present or future engagement with MFD nor shall the crew member disclose or exchange any information about the film, the script or characters or production or its pre-production and research with the public either verbally or in writing without the specific permission of MFD in writing.

10. The crew member shall not without the consent in writing of MFD incur any liabilities or debts, or claims on behalf of or against MFD nor pledge MFD's credit.

11. The crew member acknowledges that he/she shall have no copyright whatsoever in any matter concerning the film, notwithstanding the crew member's participation in the production of the film and the full rights of the film will remain solely with MFD. Furthermore, the crew member shall not be entitled to any royalties whatsoever nor share of any earnings gross or net received by MFD for the film from its distribution or sale or any other benefit of any kind derived from the film other than the salary referred to in this contract.

12. MFD may at its discretion insure against loss arising from the crew member's inability to perform his/her obligations and services hereunder but MFD shall not be liable to the crew member for any injury or damage to the crew member's person against which MFD cannot insure but MFD shall not require the crew member to render services of a hazardous or dangerous nature or which involves the crew member in an unreasonable degree of risk. MFD shall not be liable to the crew member for loss of or damage to the crew member's property brought into the studio or on location other than property in actual use at MFD's request for the purpose of production but MFD shall supply reasonable facilities for the crew member to place all personal property under security guard supervision.

13. MFD shall have the right:

    (a) in the event of the crew member's physical or mental incapacity for a period exceeding 3 consecutive days on which his/her services are required hereunder by notice in writing to suspend the operation of this agreement during the period of incapacity without making any payment to the crew member during the period of suspension or at MFD's sole and entire option, to terminate this agreement on payment to the artist of the salary due at the date of termination.

(b)   in the event of the crew member's misconduct in relation to performance of his/her duties hereunder or of his/her unwillingness to perform the services required of him/her or to fulfill the terms of this agreement, to terminate this agreement by notice in writing setting out the cause of termination and sent within 24 hours thereof upon payment to the crew member of the salary due at the date of termination.

14. If MFD shall be prevented with proceeding with the production of the film by reason of force majeure, act of God, strike, bankruptcy, lockout, fire, riot, civil commotion, national calamity, order of the public authority, enemy action or steps taken to repel same or any other cause beyond the control of MFD (excluding any risk against which insurance can reasonably be effected) MFD shall be entitled:

(a)   if production is suspended to suspend the operation of this agreement during the period of suspension of production in which case upon resumption of work on the film this agreement shall again come into effect;

(b)   if production ceases completely to terminate this agreement as from the cessation of production by notice in writing within 48 hours of termination; **provided** that if the period of suspension referred to above shall be prolonged for more than 3 days the crew member shall be entitled to work elsewhere protem, and **provided** also that if the period of suspension shall continue for more than 3 consecutive weeks either party shall be entitled to give the other written notice forthwith to terminate this agreement.

15. No waiver by MFD of any breach of any condition of this agreement by the crew member shall be deemed to be a waiver of the rights arising from any other or subsequent breach of the same or any other provision of this agreement.

16. All notices to be served by either party hereunder shall be given in writing and sent by registered post to the office in Harare of MFD or the last known address of the crew member.

17. (a)   Any disputes in question whatsoever which may arise between MFD and the crew member touching this agreement or the conditions of employment or the construction or application thereof or of any clause or thing herein contained or the rights, duties or liabilities of the parties concerned shall be referred to arbitration which shall be informally held and as expeditiously as possible.

(b)   The arbitrator shall be an independent practicing accountant of not less than 10 years' standing or a practicing legal practitioner of not less than 10 years' standing appointed by MFD. Arbitration shall be held at a venue and in accordance with formalities and/or procedures determined by the arbitrator and may be held in an informal and summary manner on the basis that it shall not be necessary to observe or carry out the usual formalities or procedure, pleadings and or discovery or the strict rules of evidence.

(c)   The arbitrator shall be entitled to investigate or cause to investigate any matter or fact or thing which he considers necessary or desirable in connection with the dispute and for that purpose he shall have the widest powers of investigating the matter and shall decide the dispute according to what he considers just and equitable in the circumstances. The arbitration shall be held as quickly as possible after it is demanded in writing with a view to its being completed within 10 days after it has been so demanded.

18. Any awards that may be made by the arbitrator shall be final and binding; will be carried into effect and may be made an order of any court to whose jurisdiction the parties to this dispute are subject.

SIGNED at HARARE this _____ day of _____ in the presence of the undersigned witnesses.

AS WITNESSES: AS WITNESSES:

1 ....   1 ....

2 ....   2 ....

Signed below for MFD   Signed below by Employee

....

About the Authors

Esta de Fossard is Senior Communication Advisor at the Johns Hopkins University's Bloomberg School of Public Health, Center for Communication Programs. She previously taught at the universities of Southern California and Ohio, as well as George Mason University in Virginia. De Fossard has been working in the field of behavior change communication for more than 30 years and has served as an international freelance consultant for numerous projects using radio or television for behavior change or classroom education. Her role involves assisting with curriculum design, training, production, and evaluation of the media campaign. Her practical experience in using media for behavior change spans 60 countries in Asia, Africa, and Latin America. She is also a prolific author with more than 50 books—both for adults and children—to her credit. Among them are the previous book in this series—*Writing and Producing Radio Dramas*—and the forthcoming book in the series—*Distance Learning via Radio, Television and the Internet.*

John Riber is an independent filmmaker and Founder–Director of the Media for Development Trust, currently based in Dar-es-Salaam, Tanzania. He has extensive experience of filmmaking in various countries of Asia and Africa. In the capacity of a communications consultant, Riber has designed and run formal film, video, and radio training courses in Asia, Africa, and the United States of America. He has also conducted research and prepared reports on the film, video, and television sectors in the southern African region.